Theology 101
in Bite-Size Pieces

*A Bird's Eye View of the Riches
of Divine Grace*

OTHER BOOKS BY JUDY AZAR LEBLANC:

Things My Father Never Taught Me
The Compromise
The Unveiling
Many Faces to Many Places

AWARDS:

2008 National Indie Excellence
2007 Reader Views Literary Choice
2006 USA Book News

THEOLOGY 101 IN BITE-SIZE PIECES

A Bird's Eye View of the Riches of Divine Grace

Judy Azar LeBlanc

WestBow
PRESS
A DIVISION OF THOMAS NELSON

WestBow Press books may be ordered through booksellers or by contacting:

WestBow Press
A Division of Thomas Nelson
1663 Liberty Drive
Bloomington, IN 47403
www.westbowpress.com
1-(866) 928-1240

Because of the dynamic nature of the Internet, any Web addresses or links contained in this book may have changed since publication and may no longer be valid. The views expressed in this work are solely those of the author and do not necessarily reflect the views of the publisher, and the publisher hereby disclaims any responsibility for them.

ISBN: 978-1-4497-0706-4 (sc)
ISBN: 978-1-4497-0707-1 (hc)
ISBN: 978-1-4497-0727-9 (e)

Library of Congress Control Number: 2010938926

Unless otherwise indicated, Scripture taken from the New American Standard Bible®, © Copyright 1960, 1962, 1963, 1968, 1971, 1972, 1973, 1975, 1977, 1995 by The Lockman Foundation. Used by permission. (www.Lockman.org)

Scripture quotations identified by Scofield are taken from the Scofield Reference Bible, © Copyright 1909, 1917; copyright renewed 1937, 1945 by Oxford University Press, Inc.

Printed in the United States of America

WestBow Press rev. date: 10/22/2010

"I will give Thee thanks forever, because Thou hast done it"
(Psalm 52:9).

This book is a compilation of the characteristics of God's gift of divine grace in bite-size pieces. The intent is to focus on Him; His attributes; His character; His nature; His disposition; and the riches of His divine grace with the hope that a deeper understanding and profound appreciation for Him may be gained from it.

CONTENTS

PREFACE

What is this thing that everyone calls "love?" Is it an emotion? Is it a commitment? Is it a phenomenon? Is it an ideal created by mankind? Does it exist at all, or is it only in our minds? Is it a hope, a dream, or a wish, or is it just a word in the dictionary? Is it God? Is there a God? Is it the energy in the universe? Do plants and animals seek it or is it only humanity who hungers for it. Some say that the only way to enter the kingdom of heaven is through love. Could this be true? How can we prove there is even a kingdom of heaven? Do we make our own kingdom of heaven on earth through love or is the kingdom of heaven simply the absence of hell and hell the absence of love? Is hell broken dreams, broken vows, broken hearts and broken wings? Are we meant to know love in its fullest or are we all born broken souls crippled from birth and sent here for repair?

What is it about this little four-letter word that stirs up such extreme emotions, and creates so many songs and movies in every imaginable language, that universally touches the human heart in such a way that it makes each and every one of us hunger for it? What is it about this little four-letter word that holds such power that it makes one capable of making the impossible become possible? What is it about this word that the very utterance of it, or lack thereof, creates such unimaginable atrocities and yet can move one's heart to the other extreme and create such peace, joy, and harmony that fill one's spirit so full that it makes us feel as though we can no longer stand the fullness of the joy? Are we even capable of knowing and feeling the fullness of the true nature of love? What is it about this little powerful word that is at the very foundation of all existence and has the power either to make us or to break us? These are the questions that some of the greatest philosophers in history have attempted to answer over the centuries, and we are still asking these very same questions today; still searching and yearning for this elusive ideology.

In both the Old and the New testaments, love is a direct command from God. "And you shall love the LORD your God with all your heart and with all your soul and with all your might. And these words, which I am commanding you today, shall be on your heart" (Deuteronomy 6:5–6). Jesus added to this commandment in John 13:34, "A new commandment I give to you, that you love one another." Jesus included this new commandment in Mark 12 when He answered the scribe who overheard the Sadducees arguing with Him about the law and went to Jesus and asked Him, "What commandment is the foremost of all?" Jesus answered, "And you shall love the Lord your God with all your heart, and with all your soul, and with all your mind, and with all your strength. The second is this, 'You shall love your neighbor as yourself.' There is no other commandment greater than these" (vv. 28–31).

But how does one love someone simply by a command? Doesn't this make us somewhat of a robot and wouldn't this then become obedience and not love? Have you ever tried to make your heart love someone or make someone else love you? I have, and I couldn't do it. In fact, the more I tried, the more resentful I became because I was doing something that I "had" to do, regardless of whether I wanted to or not. The irony is that I ended up disliking the person who I was trying so hard to love, which created more resentment in me because I was masking my feelings by being nice while at the same time was angry at her for making me feel guilty and resentful! *Surely this can't be what God meant when He gave us the command*, I thought. *Else He would have simply said, "Be nice to one another!"* I concluded that a false outward expression of love that stems from an inner contradiction cannot be love at all. There must be no contradiction. The outward expression of love must be a genuine act that stems from the heart of love, or it is not a true act of love.

Someone once told me that in order to know the difference between a genuine diamond and a cubic zirconium is not by studying the cubic zirconium, but by studying the features of a true diamond. John 3:16 says, "For God so loved the world that He gave His only begotten Son that whosoever believes in Him shall be saved." God isn't talking about the kind of limited and conditional type of cubic zirconium love that we learned, and He's not just talking about an unconditional love for humanity. He's talking about a love so great that it includes everything in the entire "Cosmos." When I think about what kind of love this is, I am unable to fully comprehend it. I was taught that *if* I wanted to be loved, *then* I had to be "loveable"; but what if I didn't feel loveable? I tried this too and discovered that *if* I didn't behave "loveably," *then* everyone would turn their back on me. I myself am guilty of doing the very same thing. Giving unconditional love doesn't come easily because it isn't in our nature to do so. If it were, then why would God have to command us to do something that would be naturally part of our own human nature? Moreover, if it was innate, then there would be no reason why we would have to be taught how to love one another or learn the difference between right and wrong. The Ten Commandments given to Moses in the Old Testament give us a clear picture of what our own nature is truly like. Scripture calls this fallen nature, sin nature, and in Ephesians 2 Paul speaks of it as the flesh.

Strong's Concordance defines the word *love* in both Hebrew and Greek using a variety of applications. For example, the word *love* as used in the Old Testament is defined as follows: *ahab*, which is translated to mean "to have a human love for another, including family, things, and a human love for God," and *chashaq,* "to be attached to or long for." The word that God uses for love in the commandment that He gave to Moses in Deuteronomy 6:5 is *ahab:* "And you shall love *(human love for God)* the LORD your God with all your heart and with all your soul and with all your might."

In the New Testament, the word *love* in the Greek language has different meanings and applications as well. The most familiar to us are *agapo* and *agape,* which are used most often throughout the New Testament. In the Greek language they are defined as "love in a social and moral sense" and love as "affection, benevolence, and charity," respectively. However, in The New American Standard New Testament Greek Lexicon (1999) hereafter referred to as the NAS Greek Lexicon, *agapo* is defined as (a) of relating to persons: "to welcome, to entertain, to be fond of, and to love dearly"; (b) of things: "to be well pleased, to be contented at or with a thing." What is interesting to note is the word that Jesus uses in giving His second commandment in John 15:12 and in Mark 12:31 is not *agape,* but *agapo.* "This is my commandment, that you *agapo* (welcome, entertain, be fond of, and love dearly) one another just as I have loved you." *Phileo,* on the other hand, is used very little in the New Testament; it is translated as "to approve, like, show signs of love, or to be fond of doing."

A good example of this is used by Paul in his letter to Titus: "All who are with me greet you. Greet those who love (*phileo*) us in the faith" (3:15). Apparently Peter had difficulty with understanding the word *love* as well. In John 21, Jesus asks Peter three times if he loved Him. What is interesting to note is that the first two times that Jesus asks Peter if he loves Him, Jesus uses the term *agapo,* and each time that Peter answers Jesus he uses the term *phileo* (vv. 15–16). Then Peter is hurt that Jesus asks him a third time, but this time Jesus also uses the term *phileo,* which is when Peter replies, "Lord, You know all things; You know that I love You" (v. 17). In light of the fact that *phileo* is rarely used in the New Testament, I tend to think that Peter didn't quite understand the depth of the question that Jesus was asking him. I have often wondered if Christ asked Peter this question on behalf of God the Father, God the Son, and God the Holy Spirit, or if it was in connection to His foreknowledge of Peter's three denials of knowing Him (Luke 22), or both.

Finally, although it is not in Scripture, another word for *love* that is quite familiar to us is *eros,* which finds its roots in the name of the classical mythological Greek god of love. This kind of love leans heavily upon the physical side of gratification. However, the best explanation that I've ever found is in 1 Corinthians 13. Paul gives us a clear picture of what the qualities of true love are: "Love is patient, love is kind. It does not envy, it does not boast, it is not proud. It is not rude, it is not self-seeking, it is not easily angered, it keeps no record of wrongs. Love does not delight in evil but rejoices with the truth. It always protects, always trusts, always hopes, always perseveres" (vv. 4–17). Like a diamond, all of the distinguishing features of love taught in both testaments are facets that make up the whole concept of true love.

How about the word *grace?* What exactly does it mean? How is it defined? What does it encompass? What are the features of it? To me it's another one of those words like *love.* As Christians, we hear this word daily. In some circles it's almost like a cliché. We are saved by grace and not by works, is what Paul taught the Ephesians in chapter 2:8–9: "By grace you are saved through faith; not of yourselves: it is a 'gift' of God, not of works, lest any man should boast." I read these words and say, yes but *what* is it? Like love, I learned this word by rote as well, but I had never actually contemplated the real meaning of either one of them. What do the words *love* and *grace really* mean? When I asked myself these questions, I honestly couldn't give myself clear and succinct answers without going to the dictionary. Yet we use these words daily, and we do so without thinking about whether or not we really mean them. I myself am guilty of this. Unlike love, grace is not a command from God. On the contrary, Scripture tells us that it is a gift from Him. I found over 266 references to grace in both the Old and the New testaments, and in both cases the definition in *Strong's Concordance* in Hebrew (*chen*) and Greek (*charis*) means "kindness and favor."

Two of the most comprehensive definitions I found, however, are from the NAS Greek Lexicon and a Merriam-Webster dictionary. The NAS Greek Lexicon defines grace (*charis*) as follows:

1. that which affords joy, pleasure, delight, sweetness, charm, loveliness: grace of speech
2. good will, loving-kindness, favor
   a. of the merciful kindness by which God, exerting his holy influence upon souls, turns them to Christ, keeps, strengthens, increases them in Christian faith, knowledge, affection, and kindles them to the exercise of the Christian virtues
3. what is due to grace
   a. the spiritual condition of one governed by the power of divine grace
   b. the token or proof of grace, benefit
      1. a gift of grace
      2. benefit, bounty
4. thanks (for benefits, services, favors), recompense, reward

Merriam-Webster also defines grace as "favor" and adds the following comprehensive definition as well: "Unmerited divine assistance given man for his regeneration or sanctification; a state of sanctification enjoyed through divine grace; a virtue coming from God."

Studying definitions can be a very tedious part of information to digest. But when I put them all together and meditate on them as a whole, they clearly reveal that divine grace is not some elusive concept that is hard to comprehend. On the contrary, it is an integral part of God's own character and is *His* own disposition of having the nature to show loving kindness, mercy, compassion and love toward mankind. Needless to say, by the time I was finished with my quest to dig deeper into understanding more about God and what His love and the gift of divine grace actually meant, I was filled with genuine joy, gratitude, and a much deeper understanding of God's love and what it cost Him to provide His divine grace for us. I visualized Him giving me a coat that was woven with different colors of thread; each thread represented a separate element of His gift of divine grace and the coat was held together by a single silver cord. Unlike putting on a coat from my own closet, when God wrapped His coat of many colors around me it became weightless and invisible, and each time that He wanted to show me a particular element of His nature, a single colored thread was highlighted in the coat.

In my mind, the difference between imparting information and receiving revelation is that without information there can be no revelation. One of my favorite Scriptures is Romans 12:2: "And do not be conformed to this world, but *be transformed by the renewal of your mind*, that you would prove what the will of God is, that which is good and acceptable and perfect." It is my sincere hope that I can communicate in layman's terms what I have learned about God's love and His gift of grace, and do so in such a way that by the time you finish reading this book you may also have a deeper understanding, appreciation, and gratitude for God's love and His gift of divine grace, and that it will strengthen your faith as it did mine.

CHAPTER 1
Back to Square One

"Before I formed you in the womb I knew you"
(Jeremiah 1:5).

When I try to wrap my mind around these words that God spoke to the prophet Jeremiah, I was unable to fully grasp them. The idea that He *foreknew* me before the foundation of the world, called me by *my* name, and predestined me to be with Him eternally, took my breath away. And He not only spoke these words to Jeremiah, but He spoke them to Isaiah as well: "Thus says the LORD who made you and formed you from the womb" (Isaiah 44:2). The apostle Paul was fully aware of this as well. In both Romans and Ephesians he wrote, "For whom he foreknew, He also predestinated to become conformed to the image of his Son" (Romans 9:29) and "Just as He chose us in Him before the foundation of the world, that we should be holy and blameless before Him in love, He predestinated us to adoption as sons through Jesus Christ to Himself, according to the kind intention of His will" (Ephesians 1:4–5).

Someone once told me that in order to see where you are going, you must look back to see from where you came. In order for me to even try to comprehend the true value of these profound words, I had to go back to the time that I first met God, revisit everything that I had been taught about Him, and question whether my belief system was based on my understanding of truth, or whether I was simply parroting someone else's words. It is like waking up one morning and realizing that, after being married for thirty years, somewhere along the line complacency had set in and you had only been going through the motions. Then it hits you—the realization of all of what you thought you knew to be true about your partner was not all true after all.

It reminded me of an old story that I once heard about a young newlywed husband who, while watching his wife make a meatloaf, saw her cut off both ends of the meat before putting it into the pan. When he questioned her about why she did so, the young wife replied, "Because this is how my mother taught me how to do it." This left the young husband perplexed enough that when he next saw his mother-in-law he asked her the same question; and she gave him the same reply. Finally, one day while he and his wife were visiting her grandmother, he asked her the same question. The grandmother replied, "We used to cut off both ends of the meat because we didn't have a pan that was big enough for it."

Even after remembering this story, I still felt a twinge of guilt for questioning what I had been taught about God. I felt like a doubting Thomas. Then late one evening while I was quietly sitting outside meditating on God, I heard a loving whisper say to me, "I want you to know Me better." For weeks my mind found no rest from hearing these words. The question that I kept asking Him was, "Lord, how am I supposed to know You better when it is You who reveals Yourself to man?" Then one evening, as I was searching my mind for an answer to this question, I was lovingly reminded about how touched I felt after I read about the doubt that Thomas had when he was told by the other apostles that they had seen the resurrected Christ. He responded by saying: "Unless *I* shall see in His hands the imprint of the nails, and put *my* finger into the place of the nails, and put *my* hand into his side, *I* will not believe" (John 20:25). According to verse 26, eight days passed before Christ returned and then, in verse 27, He said to Thomas, "Reach here your finger, and see my hands; and reach here your hand, and put it into My side; and be not unbelieving, but believing." It was then that Thomas believed and said, "My Lord and My God" (John 20:28). God knew exactly what it would take for Thomas to believe, and He met him where he was, without criticizing or rejecting him.

Thus I began to revisit and contemplate what I thought I knew about the nature and character of God, and what each one of His divine attributes really meant. But like Thomas, *I* wanted to go straight to the Word of God myself, and unless I was taught by the Holy Spirit Himself through revelation, I continued to question everything. I went so far as to question the validity of the Scriptures themselves! How would I ever know that what I was studying was even true? This question alone sent me on a long journey into an investigation of the validity of the canonization and the inspiration of the Scriptures themselves! Then, one morning, while I was prayerfully communing with God, He spoke to me through Isaiah 30:20–21: "Although the Lord has given you bread of deprivation and water of oppression, He your Teacher will no longer hide himself, but your eyes will behold your Teacher. And your ears will hear a word behind you, this is the way, walk in it, whenever you turn to the right or to the left." My heart was filled with joy for it was then that I knew that the eyes and the ears of my heart would be opened to receive a deeper understanding of God.

GOD'S OMNIPOTENCE

"For the LORD of hosts has planned, and who can frustrate it? And as for His stretched-out hand, who can turn it back?"
(Isaiah 14:27).

The record of the journeys of the Hebrews after they left the land of Egypt under the leadership of Moses is found in Numbers 33. In particular, verse 4 refers back to the judgments that God had executed upon all of the Egyptian gods that are recorded in the book of Exodus. The details given in chapters 7–11 tell how the Egyptians helplessly stood by as God executed the judgments that rendered all of their gods completely powerless to save them. I love what Isaiah wrote about God's omnipotence in Isaiah 43:13. "Even from eternity I am He; and there is *'none'* who can deliver out of my hand; I act and who can reverse it?" What is also interesting to note is that today Egypt is now considered to be a third world country.

The word *omni* comes from the Latin word *omnis* and means "all and everywhere." God is all-powerful, all-knowing, and everywhere at the same moment in time, as we know it, and in eternity past, present, and future. I don't know if one can separate each of God's attributes and categorize them as individual parts because they are all part of His character that functions together as a whole.

Genesis chapter 1 reveals three great creative acts of God.

He created the heavens and the earth (v. 1); and both animal and human life (vv. 21, 26–27) consecutively. As Genesis 2:1 states, "The heavens and the earth were finished." *Strong's Concordance* uses the word *shameh* to translate the Hebrew word *heavens* as "the visible arch in which the clouds move, as well as the higher ether where the *celestial bodies* revolve." When I consider this broader sphere of reality, I realize that just because the invisible cannot be seen, it does not mean that it does not exist. Both the prophet Isaiah and the worshippers in the Psalms recognized God's omnipotence and were awed by it. Psalm 148 specifically outlines that which God created in the universe, both in the visible and invisible world, which was done by one simple command by God. Now that's what I call power! Paul also acknowledged His omnipotence: "For by Him were all things created, which are in heaven, and which are in earth, visible and invisible, whether they be thrones, or dominions, or principalities, or powers; all things were created by Him and for Him" (Colossians 1:16).

One of my favorite theologians is Dr. Lewis Sperry Chafer, and in one of his volumes of *Systematic Theology* he assigns the heavenly hosts as follows: "Thrones to those who sit upon them, dominions to those who rule, principalities to those who govern, powers to those who exercise supremacy, and authorities to those invested with imperial responsibility" (volume 2, page 17), which suggests that the universe is not a chaotic happenstance but rather is a highly organized form of divine government. So, who are those who sit upon the thrones, and who are those principalities, powers, rulers, and authorities whose abode is in the heavenly places as recorded in Romans 8:38, Ephesians 3:10 and 6:12, and Colossians 1:16? Christ gave us this answer. He tells us in Mark 13:32 that the angel's abode is in heaven.

As a child, I was taught that we each had our own guardian angel watching over us which had always been a very comforting thought. However, it also happened to be another one of those beliefs that I had never questioned. As I scoured the Scriptures looking for some evidence to confirm this belief, I came across well over 275 references regarding angels in general and their activity. I never did find any specifics about whether or not we each had our own guardian angel, but what I did find was much more powerful. Eerdman's *International Standard Bible Encyclopedia* (Volume A-D, 1979, page 125, edited by Geoffrey W. Bromiley) gives us a clearer understanding of the distinguishing features between the angels in Scripture as revealed in both the Old Testament and the New Testament, which includes their nature, appearances, and functions. In particular, special reference is made to the "Angel of the LORD (all capital letters) and the Angel of God" as a visible manifestation of a deity to a human person. This angel is spoken of as the "angel of the presence (or face) of Yahweh." Of this same distinguishing feature, Dr. Scofield in his Bible commentary writes:

> "In the Old Testament, the expression 'the angel of the LORD' (sometimes of God) usually implies the presence of Deity in angelic form (Gen. 16.1–13; 21. 17–19; 22. 11–16; 31. 11–13; Ex. 3. 2–4; Jud. 2. 1; 6. 12–16; 13. 3–22)" (p. 1291).

Eerdman's *International Standard Bible Encyclopedia* also references where this particular angel appears to man: The angel and Hagar (Genesis 16:7–11); Abraham intercedes with the angel for Sodom (Genesis. 18); the angel who intervenes to prevent the sacrifice of Isaac (Genesis 22:11); Abraham sends Eliezar and promises him the angel's protection (Genesis 24:7, 40); the angel who appears to Jacob and says, "I am the God of Bethel" (Genesis 31:11); Jacob wrestles with the angel and says, "I have seen God face to face" (Genesis 32:24); Jacobs speaks of God and the angel as identical (Genesis 48:15); the angel who appears to Moses in the burning bush (Exodus 3); God or the angel leads Israel out of Egypt (Exodus 13:21, 14:19; Numbers 20:16); the people are commanded to obey the angel (Exodus 23:20); Moses pleads for the presence of God with His people (Exodus 32:34–33:19; Isaiah 63:9); the angel who appears to Joshua (Joshua 5:13, 6:2); the angel who speaks to the people (Judges 2:1–5); and the angel who appears to Gideon (Judges 6:11). (Eerdman's *International Standard Bible Encyclopedia*, Volume A-D, 1979, p. 125, ed. Geoffrey W. Bromiley).

In addition to the above-quoted references regarding this significant distinguishing feature, we also learn from Numbers 22 that Balaam met the angel of the LORD who blocked the path of his donkey and who also caused it to speak (vv. 22–35). 2 Chronicles mentions that Hezekiah was delivered from the Assyrian army by *one single* angel. "And the LORD sent an angel, which cut off all the mighty men of valor, and the leaders and captains in the camp of the king of Assyria" (32:21). And 2 Kings gives us more detail about this impressive feat. "And it came to pass that night, that the angel of the LORD went out and smote in the camp of the Assyrians a hundred fourscore and five thousand: and when they arose early in the morning, behold, they were all dead corpses" (19:35). That approximates 185,000 Assyrian soldiers! The angel of the LORD appears to Zorah's wife, Manoah, to tell her of the birth of Samson: "Then the angel of the LORD appeared to the woman, and said to her, 'Behold now, you are barren and have borne no children, but you shall conceive and give birth to a son'" (Judges 13:3–5). The following passages tell of the angel of God returning a second time to speak to them together (vv. 9–20).

Finally, of the few references of this visible manifestation of a deity to a human person in Scripture, two of the most remembered are the preservation of Shadrach, Meshach, and Abednego when they were thrown in the fiery furnace by King Nebuchadnezzar (Daniel 3:20–26), and the experience of Daniel when he was thrown in the lion's den (Daniel 6:16). With respect to Shadrach, Meshach, and Abednego, the following was written by Dr. J. Dwight Pentecost:

> "The men who had been tied were walking around in the furnace, unbound. And instead of seeing three men in the furnace, he (King Nebuchadnezzar) saw four and he said the fourth was like a son of the gods. This one was probably the preincarnate Christ and though Nebuchadnezzar did not know of the Son of God, he did recognize that the Person appearing with the three looked supernatural" *(The Bible Knowledge Commentary*, 1983, p. 1340).

And of Daniel's preservation when he was thrown into the lion's den (Daniel 6:16–23), Dr. Pentecost commented:

> "God's Angel, Daniel said, had kept the lions' mouths shut. Perhaps this Angel, like the One in the fiery furnace with the three young men (3:25), was the preincarnate Christ" (Ibid., p. 1349).

Of other angels whose particular features and activities are recorded, I began with the cherubim and seraphim because they seem to be angels of a higher order which are specifically called by those titles in Scripture. What I found most interesting is that the seraphim are only mentioned once in Scripture, and that is done by Isaiah in 6:2–3. In his vision, Isaiah describes what they look like, what he saw them doing, and what he heard them saying: "Seraphim stood above Him, each having six wings; with two he covered his face and with two he covered is feet, and with two he flew. And one called out to another and said, 'Holy, Holy, Holy, is the LORD of Hosts; the whole earth is full of His glory.'"

Cherubim on the other hand are mentioned a bit more often. Beginning in Genesis they appear as *guardians* of the tree of life (3:24), and in Ezekiel's complicated vision, he describes each one having four faces and four wings with human-like hands underneath their wings (10:21). Then in Exodus 25, we learn that God gave Moses exact instructions for making the cherubim who were a part of the construction of the ark, including the dimensions, material, location of where he was to place them, and the exact position that he was to place them in. "And the cherubim shall have their wings spread upward, covering the mercy seat with their wings and facing one another; the faces of the cherubim are to be turned toward the mercy seat" (vv. 18–20). Symbolic of guardianship, King Solomon also sculptured cherubim and placed them in the middle of the sanctuary of the temple that he built. (1 Kings 6:23–38; 2 Chronicles 3:11–14).

Out of all of the different occasions that are referenced in both the old and new testaments, where God sent His angels to intercede on behalf of man either as messengers or as warriors, the two most notable are Michael and Gabriel. Michael is the only archangel whose name, title, position, and activity are revealed to us, and he is mentioned only five times in both the Old and New testaments. Jude 9 specifically identifies him as "Michael the archangel," and Revelation 12:7 tells us that Michael is a great warrior. "And there was war in heaven, Michael and his angels waging war with the dragon. And the dragon and his angels waged war." What I found comforting was the very next verse tells us that the dragon and his angels lost the war!

"And they were not strong enough, and there was no longer a place found for them in heaven." Of Michael's other titles and activities, Daniel identifies him as "Michael, *one* of the chief princes came to help me" (10:13), which suggests that there are more archangels. And in the last words in verse 21, Michael is identified as "Michael your prince," which is translated in *Strong's Concordance* to mean *arche*. Finally, in chapter 12, Daniel states, "Michael, the great prince *(arche)* who stands guard over the sons of your people, will arise" (v. 1). When I think about someone being a prince, I think of someone earthly like Prince Charles of the British royal family. I certainly don't think of an angel who is as powerful as Michael, the great *arche*.

Gabriel on the other hand is apparently a messenger for God and his activities are quite different from those of Michael's. He is only mentioned twice by name in the Old Testament. Daniel tells us in chapter 8 that Gabriel was sent to him to interpret his vision. "And I heard the voice of a man between the banks of the Ulai, and he called out and said, 'Gabriel, give this man an understanding of the vision'" (v. 16). The verses that immediately follow are Gabriel's interpretation of that vision for Daniel. Then Gabriel is sent to give Daniel a message a second time in chapter 9 while Daniel is still praying. "While I was still speaking in prayer, then the man Gabriel, whom I had seen in the vision previously, came to me in my extreme weariness about the time of the evening offering. And he gave me instruction and talked with me, and said, 'O Daniel, I have now come forth to give you insight with understanding'" (vv. 21–22).

In the New Testament, Gabriel is only mentioned twice by name as well. In chapter 1, the great historian Luke records that Gabriel was sent to give a message to Zacharias and to Mary, and in both cases the message was to announce the birth of a son (vv. 19–38). Gabriel's message to Zacharias is so detailed that he not only tells Zacharias what to name his son, but outlines six aspects of what his son's character will be like (vv. 13–17). After Zacharias questions the angel, Gabriel then identifies himself by saying, "I am Gabriel, who stands in the presence of God; and I have been sent to speak to you, and to bring you this good news" (vv. 18–19).

Both Daniel and John had wonderful revelation given to them in visions of these majestic and powerful beings which God created. "A river of fire was flowing and coming out from before Him; Thousands upon thousands were attending Him, And ten thousand times ten thousand were standing before Him; The court sat, And the books were opened" (Daniel 7:10). That is a lot of angels! John spoke of the angels' activities from chapter 14 to chapter 22 in the book of Revelation, and we know that this is true because in the last chapter, Jesus himself verified what John saw: "I, Jesus, have sent My angel to testify to you these things for the churches. I am the root and offspring of David, the bright morning star" (v. 16).

When I think about all of this unceasing activity that is occurring in the "invisible" world, I cannot even imagine the kind of supernatural power that these angels have been given by our Creator. David spoke about their strength and obedience in Psalm 103:20. Of the unnamed angels that appear throughout Scripture who carry out a variety of tasks for God, we know that when Lot and his family were living in Sodom and Gomorrah, God sent two of His angels to take them out of the city and to guide them to safety before He completely destroyed it (Genesis 19:1–22). When the prophet Elijah feared for his life and fled into the wilderness, an angel was sent to provide him with food and water (1 Kings 19:6–7).

Angels were quite active in the New Testament as well. When Joseph secretly planned to divorce Mary after he discovered that she was pregnant, an angel was sent to him in a dream to reassure him that Mary had not been unfaithful, and to tell him about the birth of Jesus (Matt. 1:20–23); after Satan tempted Jesus in the wilderness, angels were sent to minister to Him (Matthew 4:11); while Jesus was agonizing in the Garden of Gethsemane, an angel was sent to strengthen Him (Luke 22:43–44). Matthew also records that while the Romans were guarding the tomb where Jesus was lying, an angel came and rolled away the stone: "And behold, a severe earthquake had occurred, for an angel of the Lord descended from heaven and came and rolled away the stone and sat upon it. And his appearance was like lightning, and his garment as white as snow; and the guards shook for fear of him and became like dead"

(28:2–4). After the crucifixion, two angels appeared to the women who first discovered the empty tomb to tell them that Jesus had risen (Luke 24:4–6). Chapters 5 and 12 of the book of Acts records two different occasions when God sent an angel to release the apostles from prison; an angel was sent to Philip to give him a message (8:26); and Luke records that Jesus Himself tells us that angels carried the spirit of Lazarus to Abraham's bosom when he died (6:22). These are only a few of the several occasions that angels were sent on behalf of man that are recorded throughout Scripture.

With respect to whether or not I found any scriptural evidence of having a particular guardian angel assigned to me, I did not. However, I was much more comforted to know that God has not charged just one of His angels, but He charged several of them to guard me as recorded in Psalm 91. "For He will give His angels charge concerning you, to guard you in all your ways; they will bear you up in their hands, lest you strike your foot against a stone" (vv. 11–12). As I read these words that the psalmist wrote, I was reminded of an incident that once occurred while I was on the freeway. I was following an open-ended pickup that was driving at the speed of about seventy-five miles per hour. The back end of his truck was piled high with eight-foot long, two-by-four-inch pieces of wood when one of them suddenly flew off and headed straight for my windshield. In that moment, I didn't know if I had enough time to change lanes before it hit, but as I did, I watched that two-by-four hang in the air long enough for me to safely make a lane change before it hit the roadway. I have often wondered about what might have happened to me that day had that two-by-four not miraculously come to a curt halt in mid-air.

GOD'S OMNIPRESENCE

What has always been so impressive to me about the men of God in the Old Testament is that they knew so much about Him. Throughout the Old Testament they write about all of His attributes, His nature and His character. I often muse over the thought that they did not go to church every Sunday and they were not seminary graduates. What it does show is that they were men who loved God, believed in Him, spent untold time communing with Him, and were taught by the God Most High, God Himself. In chapter 139, the psalmist writes about God's omnipresence with this profound thought in mind: *"Where can I go from Thy Spirit? Or where can I flee from Thy presence? If I ascend to heaven, Thou are there; if I make my bed in Sheol, behold, Thou are there. If I take the winds of the dawn, if I dwell in the remotest part of the sea, even there Thy hand will lead me and Thy right hand will lay hold of me"* (vv. 7–10).

CHAPTER 2
God's Omniscience

"Thine eyes have seen my unformed substance; And in Thy Book they were all written, the days that were ordained for me, when as yet there was not one of them" (Psalm 139:16).

Foreknown, Predestinated, and Called

The thought of being foreknown, predestinated, and called is a concept that is quite difficult for me to wrap my mind around. On the other hand, I have also concluded that there are many things that simply go beyond human understanding. I tend to think that trying to conceptualize and understand each one of these individual parts and how each personally applies to me is much like trying to separate the divine attributes of God. Nonetheless, it sometimes serves me well to dissect a whole concept so that I can better understand how all of the individual parts together make it function as a whole. I would like to think that a good mechanic would know exactly how all of the individual parts of a car work before he takes it apart and puts it back together again.

What I have often pondered is this: Did God predestinate because He foreknew, or did He foreknow and then predestinate that which He foreknew? It's similar to the question of which came first, the chicken or the egg? I finally came to a comfortable conclusion that God couldn't predestinate what He didn't foreknow in all eternity. It would be like knowing that I had planned to have a special banquet, invited a houseful of guests, and then did absolutely nothing to prepare for it. What I tend to keep forgetting is that time as we relate to it in our daily lives is an earthly feature that includes past, present, future, seasons and ages; whereas in God's abode of eternity, time is timeless. Almost all of Psalm 139 is dedicated to the acknowledgement of being foreknown in eternity by the power of the omniscience of God. Paul was also given a clear understanding of how all of these parts work together as a whole, which he writes about in Romans 8:29–30 and in Ephesians 1:5, 11.

The word *predestinated* comes from the Greek word *proorizo*, which carries the meaning of "determine beforehand, ordain, to decide upon ahead of time." This concept of predestinated is wholly different from the secular concept of predestination which implies that no matter what you decide, the outcome has already been predetermined. During election season, I have often heard it said "If God has already determined who is going to be in power, then why bother casting my vote?" This idea not only negates the execution of man's free will to choose, but also subtly implies that God does interfere with it. As I scoured the Scriptures, I found that God's people consistently ignored His guidance, made their own choices, and paid the consequences for them. I did not find one place where God interfered with man's free will to choose. On the contrary, what I did find was that based on His foreknowledge of the choices that His people would be making, and because of His love and desire to protect them, He sent one prophet after another to remind them of all of the blessings that they would receive *if* they chose to follow His instructions, and of the consequences that they would have to endure if they chose to ignore them.

I often think about all of the grief that I caused my poor mother and what she must have gone through while raising me. I reflect upon how many times she tried to spare me from suffering the consequences that she knew I would have to endure for making the wrong choices. However, because of my rebellious temperament, and my unwillingness to follow her instructions, I continually challenged her, made the wrong choices, and suffered the consequences. I still personally struggle with the concept of predestination not only because of a lack of clear understanding of how it affects my ability to choose freely, but because of how my ego continually reminds me that because I am able to choose freely, I can choose what I want, when I want, and if I want. God certainly is not going to force me to do anything that I am not willing to do—He is not a dictator, or why would He have given us a free will at all. It wasn't until I sincerely asked God what it was that He wanted from me that He gave me a glimpse of what it means. I did not hear Him say "I want you to be my slave," or "I want you to act like a mindless robot and do everything that I ask you to do because I command it." What I did hear Him say was *"I want you to understand how much I love you"* To some, this might sound like such a simple request. However, having come from a strict "religious" background, and from a fatherless home, I was not taught that He was a God of love, but rather that He was a controlling and punishing God who was always watching to see if I made a mistake just so that He could inflict punishment on me. Naturally, under these circumstances, I rebelled against this as well. Paradoxically, however, it wasn't until I met the one and only true God that I discovered that I had spent my entire youth running away from a false God.

I oftentimes forget that it is not all about me, but that it's all about Him and who He is; and that in His omniscient power, and of His own free will and gracious nature, He took it upon Himself to save our souls from being eternally separated from Him, and that is what changed the destiny of mankind. After meditating on this fact,

I finally came to realize that predestination is not a relinquishing of man's will in making daily decisions pertaining to his life, nor is it something to be used as an excuse to do nothing because of it. This would be more like holding to the fatalistic view that God will do what He will do irrespective of your desire and regardless of what one decides either to do or not to do. Instead, it is a part of God's divine plan that He provided from the foundation of the world, which makes it possible for man to return home as revealed by Matthew in chapter 25. "Then the King will say to those on His right, 'Come, you who are blessed of My Father, inherit the kingdom *prepared for you from the foundation of the world*'" (v. 34). This not only tells me that we have been part of His mindful consideration since the beginning of creation, but also that while we are in this world, however long or short it may be, we are more than just beings having a human experience. We are spiritual beings as well. Christ did not come to teach us how be religious. I think He made Himself perfectly clear on how He felt about that. He came to redeem what rightfully belongs to Him, to *show His people the way to get back home,* and to teach us how to live as His spiritual children while we are here. I am sincerely grateful that His free will is not anything like mine.

It All Fits Together

In my early Christian walk, words, such as *called, chosen* and *elected,* were always quite mystifying to me. It wasn't until I sat down to study the differences between these words to learn how they are used in Scripture that I received a better understanding of how they fit into God's divine plan of being foreknown and predestinated. Although this may appear to be a little tedious, I believe that it is of utmost importance to show the differences in their meanings so that there is a clearer understanding of how they apply within the context of their use.

As is quite common in our own English language, a single word that has a variety of meanings becomes more easily understood within its context. With the exception of the word *called,* the words *elected* and *chosen* have the same meaning both in Hebrew and in Greek and are used interchangeably in Scripture in both the Old and New testaments. Keeping in mind that the word *called* is used in the past tense, the NAS Greek Lexicon defines it in a variety of ways. In the New Testament, the term *kletos* is found only nine times and is translated as "called, invited (to a banquet), or invited by God in the proclamation of the gospel to obtain eternal salvation in the kingdom through Christ; called to (the discharge of) some office or called as in divinely selected and appointed." For example, in his salutation in both Romans and in 1 Corinthians, Paul uses *kletos* to mean that he is a divinely selected and appointed apostle by God, whereas in Romans 8:28 he uses *kletos* to mean those who have chosen to receive the invitation by God to obtain eternal salvation through Christ.

The translation of *kletos* is not too different from that of *kaleo,* which is used most often throughout the New Testament. The NAS Greek Lexicon defines it as follows: "to call aloud, utter in a loud voice, to invite, to call by name or give a name to; to be called (to bear a name or title among men)." I found well over 125 Scriptures where this particular translation is used in a variety of ways that I have listed in Appendix G. However, the most significant Scripture where Paul uses *kaleo* within the context of being foreknown, predestinated, and called is found in Romans 8: "For whom He foreknew, He also predestinated to become conformed to the image of His Son, that He might be first-born among many brethren; and whom He predestinated, these He also called; and whom He called, these He also justified; and whom He justified, these He also glorified" (vv. 29–30).

Finally, unrelated to foreknown, predestinated, and called, and with the exception of John, both Paul and the gospel writers often use the Greek word *proskaleomai* which is translated to mean "to call to oneself or to summon. An example of where this is used can be found in Matthew 18:2: "And He called a child to Himself and set him before them." I try to keep the attribute of God's omniscient power in the forefront of my mind because when I do, then as I study and read through Scripture, it all seems to become much clearer to me. I love to meditate on the fact that God knows what I am going to choose to do before I choose to do it and has already worked all things before I have chosen. Yet should it turn out to be that some of those choices produce what seemingly appear to be bad results, what He says in Romans 8 is that He uses all things for the good for those who love Him and to those who are called according to His purpose (v. 28).

I must admit that I don't fully comprehend all of the inner workings of this truth or appreciate it to the fullest degree, but I have seen it work in my life. I reflect on one particular instance that is still quite fresh in my mind where this principle applied to my life even before I became a Christian. When I was just beginning my professional career, I was being groomed for an executive position in a well-known company in San Francisco. One morning, the vice president called me into his office to tell me that the company was planning to open a new product branch in another city. Without disclosing any further details about the project, he simply stated that I had five minutes to decide on whether or not I would join him. I was not given a moment of extra time to weigh the pros or cons of leaving, or how it would affect my career. In fact, I was not even given an idea of what my new position would be! All I was given were five minutes to make this life-changing choice. Without any further thought, I spontaneously accepted this offer.

After relocating and settling into my new home, I shortly discovered that my next-door neighbor was a born-again Christian who eventually became the one who was instrumental in leading me to Christ. The change in my career was not really the focal point of God's plan. In my case it was being placed with the right person, at the right time and place that fulfilled the part of God's perfect plan that He had for my life. Shortly thereafter, I ended up leaving the company because it turned out that the career change was not for the better after all.

RSVP Required

Based on this information, I think it is now safe to say that God "invites" (calls) all of humanity to receive salvation through the gospel, but only Christians who have already RSVP'd may be referred to as "the called." Furthermore, because of His omniscience, He personally knows all of those who have been called (i.e., those who have already accepted the invitation), all of those who are yet to accept, as well as all of those who will not, and this was known to Him in eternity past. What comes to mind is the parable that Christ tells in Matthew 22 about the king who gave a wedding feast for his son. The king sent out his slaves to call all those who had been invited to come to the feast. After they all refused, the king sent his slaves back out into the streets to invite everyone else, and verse 10 records that the wedding hall was then filled.

Mystery Solved

In my early Christian walk, my mind struggled with understanding who the chosen and the elect are that are written about throughout both the Old and the New testaments. As it turns out, according to the lexiconists Brown, Driver, Briggs, and Gesenius, and in the NAS Greek Lexicon, there are no differences between the translations of the meaning of *elect* and *chosen* in either Hebrew or in Greek. What

I discovered is that these terms are used interchangeably throughout both testaments. For example, in Isaiah 43:20 God says that He gave rivers in the desert to give drink to "His chosen people," and in 45:4 you will find that God tells Cyrus that He anointed him for the sake of Israel, "His elect." Both of these terms in Hebrew are translated *bachiyr* and are simply defined as "chosen; choice one, chosen one, elect (of God)."

The most significant Scripture in the Old Testament is the prophecy of the coming Messiah, which was planned for in eternity past, and who was predestinated, elected and chosen to be our Savior. This prophecy can be found in chapter 42: "Behold, My Servant, whom I uphold; My chosen one (elect), in whom My soul delights; I have put My Spirit upon Him; He will bring forth justice to the nations" (v. 1).

In a variety of Scripture in the New Testament, *elect* and *chosen* are equally translated *eklektos,* which is defined as "picked out; chosen by God to obtain salvation through Christ." Christians are called *chosen* or *elect* of God; the Messiah is called *elect,* as appointed by God to the most exalted office conceivable; choice, select, in other words the best of its kind or class, excellence preeminent; applied to certain individual Christians.

An example of how these are applied interchangeably can be found in Matthew 24:31 where God tells us that He will send forth His angels with a great sound of a trumpet to gather together "His elect" (chosen ones) from the four winds, and Luke 23:35 records, "And the people stood by, looking on. And even the rulers were sneering at Him, saying, He saved others; let Him save Himself if this is the Christ of God, His Chosen One."

Not related to being chosen (invited) to receive salvation, but within the same context of being predestinated and called, is being "chosen" for a specific task. A few examples of men and women whom God knew beforehand would accept tasks of their own free will are believers, such as Abraham, Isaac, Jacob, Moses, the prophets, Solomon, Saul, David, Joseph, Mary, the Apostles, and Paul.

Thus, of His own free will, Christ Himself was foreknown, predestinated, called, and elected to be our Savior in eternity past. Additionally, He also knows all of those who have already accepted His invitation, all of those who have not, and all of those who have yet to receive it.

CHAPTER 3
The Lost Estate

As Christians, we know that we have inherited a sin nature through the contaminated seed of Adam because of the fall. I like to think of it in terms of it being "the nature of the beast." However, in my line of thinking, my question became threefold: (1) *if we belonged to God in the first place, then why did we have to be brought back; (2) from whom did we have to be redeemed; and (3) if God foreknew that Adam was going to choose to disobey His command not to eat from the tree of the knowledge of good and evil, as disclosed in Genesis 2:6, and He foreknew the gravity of the consequences thereof, then why did He allow it?*

The Estate

The search for these answers led me back to the beginning of the first and last verse of Genesis 1 where it is recorded that "In the beginning, God created the heaven and the earth" (v. 1) and ends with, "And God saw all that He had made and behold, it was very good" (v. 31). The Hebrew word for heaven is *shamayim,* which is translated by Brown, Driver, Briggs, and Gesenius to be "heaven, heavens, sky; visible heavens, sky; abode of the stars; as the visible universe, the sky, atmosphere; and heaven (as the abode of God)."

This suggests that the heavens, including the heavenly hosts, were created both before earth and before the first man, Adam. The prophet Ezekiel describes Satan in the way that God had originally created him to be. He writes that Satan had a highly exalted position as an anointed cherub in God's kingdom, and that he was created with splendor, perfect in beauty, blameless, and full of wisdom (28:12–15).

Scientific evidence in a variety of fields tells us that earth is over 4 billion years old. This suggests that in some dateless period of time between the creation of the heavens and the earth when it was in that perfect form in which they first appeared (Genesis 1:1), and that period when the earth became waste and empty (Genesis 1:2; Isaiah 24:1; Jeremiah 4:23–26), Satan chose to reject God and become completely independent from him by asserting his infamous five "*I will's*" as recorded by Isaiah. "You said in your heart, *I will* ascend to heaven; *I will* raise my throne above the stars of God; *I will* sit enthroned on the mount of assembly, on the utmost heights of the sacred mountain. *I will* ascend above the tops of the clouds; *I will* make myself like the Most High" (14:12–14). In chapter 28, Ezekiel then reveals to us the motives and the consequences of that fall (vv. 16–18) and Genesis 3 gives a record of the origin and the cause of man's fall from divine grace. It reveals that first human act of disobedience is what caused spiritual death and eternal separation from God, which then was passed on to all of humanity through the corrupted seed of Adam. As a result, man is naturally born spiritually separated from God. Scripture explains this in terms of being born of the flesh as opposed to the spirit, or being naturally born with sin nature. Genesis also reveals that at some dateless point in time, the first angelic act of rebellion occurred in the heavenly sphere. The havoc that was produced in the heavens by this rebellion is what corrupted God's perfect system and gave birth to the diabolical system that we now live under.

Thus, understanding that we have inherited Adam's fallen nature as a consequence of man's first disobedient act (Genesis 3:6) that causes man to choose to be independent from God; Scripture reveals that by Satan committing the first rebellious act in the universe is what corrupted all of which God originally created as perfect and good. However, though it was anticipated by God, it was the consequences of this rebellion that created the diabolical system that we now live under. Therefore, by God commanding Adam to stay away from the tree of the knowledge of good and evil clearly indicates that evil was already present in the earth; and as we well know, the war between good and evil has long since been an ongoing battle. In my mind's eye, this was the First World War.

Panning for Gold

"In the beginning was the Word, and the Word was with God, and the Word was God ... And the Word became flesh, and dwelt among us, and we saw His glory, glory as of the only begotten from the Father, full of grace and truth" (John 1:1, 14).

I love the way God reveals little golden nuggets that are hidden throughout the Scriptures. For me, it is like taking a trip to the river to pan for gold. God's genius of the foreknowledge for the need of a plan for our salvation, and as a manifestation of His love for His creation, the completed work of the crucifixion, death, and resurrection of Christ was already prepared by Him in eternity past. This revelation is written and prophesied throughout the entire Old Testament and fulfilled in the New Testament. The first announcement that relates to this is found in the first book of Genesis and is directly aimed at the serpent. "And I will put enmity between you and the woman, and between your seed and her seed; He shall bruise you on the head, and you shall bruise him on the heel" (3:15). And His last announcement is found in the last book of Malachi and is directly aimed at His creation. "Behold, I am going to send My messenger, and he will clear the way before Me. And the Lord, whom you seek, will suddenly come to His temple; and the 'messenger of the covenant,' in whom you delight, behold, He is coming" (3:1).

The Restoration

When I thoughtfully meditate on this powerful Scripture, and on the impact that this unimaginably painful act of selfless love had on the world, I cannot help but feel overwhelmed by it. Understanding that the diabolical system was created by the first angelic rebellion led me to further investigate the meaning of the term *the world* as used throughout the New Testament. What I discovered not only impacted my understanding of the profound significance of what the crucifixion, death, and resurrection of Christ meant for the sake of humanity, but what it meant for the sake of the entire cosmos.

In the New Testament, the term "world" has three different meanings in Greek, and depending upon the context of the Scripture in which it is being used, the applications of them vary. The NAS Greek Lexicon translates the term *world* in Greek as this: (1) *cosmos,* defined as "an apt and harmonious arrangement or constitution, order, government; an ornament, decoration, adornment, the arrangement of the 'heavenly hosts' being an adornment of the heavens; the world, the universe; the earth, the inhabitants of the earth, men, the human family; the ungodly multitude; the whole mass of men alienated from God and hostile to the cause of Christ"; and finally, "world affairs, the aggregate of things earthly"; (2) *oikoumene,* "the inhabited earth; the portion of the earth inhabited by the Greeks, in distinction from the lands of the barbarians; the Roman empire; the world, the inhabitants of the earth, men; and the universe"; and

(3) *aion,* "forever, an unbroken age, perpetuity of time, eternity; the worlds, universe; period of time, age."

By the simple definition, the *world* refers to a world system ruled by the prince of darkness. In most cases the New American Standard Bible already has it properly translated to mean "age" or "the inhabited earth," otherwise it is translated to mean the "cosmos" in the fullness of the word. My reason for considering this term to be of utmost importance is because when I understood it more fully, my appreciation of the crucifixion, death, and resurrection of Christ was profoundly impacted. The word that Christ used in John 3:16–17 is *kosmos,* and its definition is all inclusive to mean His perfect creation in its *entirety* as He originally created it to be, prior to the angelic rebellion that resulted in the corruption of His perfect system. This includes the relationship that man had with God, constitution, government, and the angelic sphere. Yet in His profound prayer recorded in John 17, He said, "And yet they themselves are in the world" (v. 11a); "I have given them Thy word; and the world has hated them, because they are not of the world (*kosmos*), even as I am not of the world" (v. 14). This is meant in the context of salvation. In other words, it refers to all of those believers whose souls have been snatched out of the hands of the power of the prince of darkness that rules the diabolical system of the world are those who now belong to Him. "And I give eternal life to them, and they shall never perish; and no one shall snatch them out of My hand. My Father, who has given *them* to Me, is greater than all; and no one is able to snatch *them* out of the Father's hand. I and the Father are one" (John 10:28–30).

CHAPTER 4
The Riches of Divine Grace

"Remember Him before the silver cord is broken and the golden bowl is crushed, the pitcher by the well is shattered and the wheel at the cistern is crushed" (Ecclesiastes 12:6).

When I think about each one of the different aspects that pertain to the gift of divine grace, I think of a coat that has been uniquely woven with different colors of thread that is held together by a single silver cord. I like to think of each color of thread as being unique to each of the different features of grace that is held together by God's spirit. I also like to think of a flawless, perfectly cut diamond that when placed in the right position in the light will radiate a multitude of rich, intense, and pure colors that cannot be seen otherwise. In either case, the sum of the individual qualities together equals perfection.

The definition of the term *charis* was introduced in detail in the preface. It is a virtue belonging to God that is a part of His own character whose disposition is to have and to show loving kindness, compassion, mercy, and love toward mankind that is completely unmerited. It is also a spiritual condition of the soul that is wholly governed by the power of God's divine grace. When I was growing up I always heard the preachers say that Christ died for us sinners and that if we didn't confess our sins then we were going to go to hell. This concept led me to believe that I was nothing but a bad person and that my external behavior had everything to do with my destiny. I don't ever remember being taught that being lost meant that it is a spiritual condition of the soul, or that man is not capable of saving it himself. Neither do I remember being taught that by virtue of God's own character, not mine, He took it upon Himself to rescue man's soul from being eternally separated from Him wholly by the power of His own divine grace through the free gift of salvation. On the contrary, I was led to believe that if I sinned I would go to hell and if I didn't then I would go to heaven—the burden was laid upon my own shoulders—pure and simple. In fact, I can still recall the day when the burden became so heavy that I finally resigned myself to the idea that no matter what I did, I was going to go to hell anyway, so I said, "I'm done—if I'm going to go to hell, then I may as well enjoy the ride." Years later, after I received the "good news" to the contrary, I finally understood the words that Christ spoke to everyone when He said, "Come to Me, all who are weary and heavy-laden, and I will give you rest. Take My yoke upon you, and learn from Me, for I am gentle and humble in heart; and YOU SHALL FIND REST FOR YOUR SOULS. For My yoke is easy, and My load is light" (Matthew 11:28–30).

REDEMPTION

"I have wiped out your transgressions like a thick cloud, and your sins like a heavy mist. Return to Me, for I have redeemed you"
(Isaiah 44:22b).

As you may already know, the act of redemption is a doctrine that is written about throughout the Old Testament and fulfilled by Christ in the New. It basically means to recover ownership of something or someone by paying a specific sum. In Hebrew, Brown, Driver, Briggs, and Gesenius translate it to be *ga'al* and *padah* and both have various definitions and applications which are listed in Appendix H. However, for this purpose, the best example of the act of redemption that I have found in the Old Testament is depicted in the story of Boaz and Ruth. It tells what the legal responsibilities of a kinsman redeemer were for those who were under the law. Deuteronomy 25:5–10 reveals that this custom required a close relative to marry the widow of the deceased (the kinsman) in order to continue his family line. Although it is not explicitly written on the pages of this story, there are some striking similarities that parallel Boaz's act of redemption on behalf of Ruth, and Christ's act of redemption on behalf of His church. As the story is written, Ruth was a widowed Moabite who after marrying a Judaite became a convert; therefore she was under the Mosaic Law. Boaz however was not the nearest relative and therefore had no legal responsibility to act on behalf of Ruth as kinsman redeemer. Nonetheless, by a show of his love and grace, he found a way to fulfill the law and ultimately became her kinsman redeemer. What I also found to be enlightening is that men like the prophet Isaiah and the psalmist speak about redemption in the *past* tense. In chapter 44, the prophet writes: "I have wiped out your transgressions like a thick cloud, and your sins like a heavy mist. Return to Me, for I have redeemed you" (44:22b); and "For thus says the LORD, 'You were sold for nothing and you will be redeemed without money' (52:3). Keeping in mind that the power of redemption is in the hands of the redeemer and not in the hands of the redeemed, the price that was paid to buy back what rightfully belongs to God was the crucifixion, death, and resurrection of Christ.

In the New Testament, however, the translation of the Greek term carries a much deeper meaning. The terms *redeem* and *redeemed* are both translated as *lutroo* and defined to mean "liberate by payment of ransom; to deliver from evils of every kind, both internal and external"; *lutrosis* as "a deliverance from the penalty of sin"; and *exagorazo* to mean "of Christ freeing the elect from the dominion of the Mosaic Law at the price of his death." And since Christ did not come to abolish the law but to fulfill it (Matthew 5:17), this particular quality is peculiar to the term *redemption* in the New Testament. Therefore, the moment we receive Christ as our Lord and Savior, we are freed from the law *(exagorazo),* our souls are redeemed *(lutroo)* by our kinsman redeemer, and we are delivered from the power of the prince of darkness (the diabolical system that is hostile toward God) and transported into God's kingdom.

Personally, I like to think of it as Him paying the full price for us, thus He has full right to claim us as His own possession. As Paul so succinctly put it, "Or do you not know that your body is the temple of the Holy Spirit who is in you, whom you have from God, and that you are not your own?" (1 Corinthians 6:19).

RECONCILIATION

"For while we were enemies, we were reconciled to God through the death of His Son; much more, having been reconciled, we shall be saved by his life" (Romans 5:10).

To say that we were reconciled to God connotes that there once was harmony in the relationship between God and man. Lexiconists translate this Greek term as *katallasso* and define it to mean "*to receive one into favor or to return to favor with.*"

In Paul's message to the Corinthians, he tells them that it is God who reconciled us to Himself through His Son and explains that it was God Himself who was in Christ reconciling the "world" to Himself, and then he goes on to beg them on behalf of Christ to be reconciled to Him (2 Corinthians 5:18–20). I can't help but think of a marriage relationship whose beginnings were founded in a love that ran so deep that when it was sealed by the flesh, it created such closeness that they became one spirit bound by the heart. Then the unthinkable happens–something occurs in the relationship that causes a separation between the two. Sometimes they are able to reconcile, and sometimes they are not. However, in either case, the reconciliation can only be secured by the willingness of both parties.

God's love for His creation ran so deep in His heart that when the relationship between Himself and His creation was broken, He reconciled it by becoming flesh, bound it by the crucifixion and death of Christ, and then sealed it with His spirit by His resurrection. In his careful analysis, Dr. Chafer points out the differences between the reconciliation of the world and the reconciliation of the believer to God that Paul presented to the Corinthians. Of this he writes the following:

> "A difference will be recognized between the reconciliation of the world as declared in 5:19–and the reconciliation of the individual–as declared in 5:20–21. The reconciliation of the world does not obviate the reconciliation of the individual. The latter is that form of reconciliation which is applied to the believer's heart and results in a perfect and unending peace between God and the reconciled believer. To be perfectly reconciled to God on the ground of the merit of Christ, as it is true of every child of God, is a position of blessedness indeed and is one of the riches of God's Divine Grace" (*Systematic Theology,* volume 3, p. 236).

As in the case of all estranged relationships, to be reconciled to God now wholly depends upon the willingness of the individual to be reconciled to Him—God already did His part, now individuals must do theirs.

FORGIVENESS

"In Him we have redemption through His blood, the forgiveness of our trespasses, according to the riches of His grace, which He lavished upon us" (Ephesians 1:7–8).

When I meditate on this aspect of God's grace, I get overwhelmed by all of what is characteristic of His nature. I sometimes struggle with comprehending the fact that God has forgiven all of my transgressions past, present, and future. If it does mean that I am already forgiven for whatever transgressions I am currently committing and includes those I have yet to commit, then what did John mean when he wrote the following? "If we confess our sins, He is faithful and righteous to forgive us our sins and to cleanse us from all unrighteousness" (1 John 1:9). Having taught English at one time, I cannot help but be struck by the remembrance of so many different words that we have in our language in which one single word carries numerous definitions and conveys numerous meanings. Likewise, the word *forgiveness* in Greek carries numerous definitions that convey different meanings as well. In his writings to both the Ephesians (1:7) and to the Colossians (1:14), lexiconists point out that Paul uses the Greek word *aphesis* which means "to release from bondage or imprisonment; a pardon of sins (letting them go as if they had never been committed), and a remission of the penalty." This aspect of God's grace not only includes the forgiveness of my sins past, present, and future, but it also includes the remission of the penalty. John on the other hand uses *aphiemi,* which means "to disregard."

The seeming paradox—that I am forgiven and yet must be forgiven—was cleared up when I understood the differences between the two types of forgiveness that the different meanings convey. One relates to the kind of forgiveness that a believer receives at the moment of salvation, while the other relates to personal forgiveness *after* salvation. Paul's use of the word *aphesis* for forgiveness relates to man's permanent standing in Christ, while the one John uses, *aphiemi,* relates to man's standing within the body of Christ. Through *aphesis,* one reconciles man to God permanently, while the other reconciles broken relationships within the body of Christ and restores the broken fellowship that this creates with God. In either case, forgiveness relies on God's character in accordance with the riches of His grace (Ephesians 2:7), but the first relies completely on God to forgive, while the other relies on man to ask for forgiveness from God for personal offences committed after salvation.

Freed from the Law

"'But this is the covenant which I will make with the people of Israel after those days,' declares the LORD,'I will put My law within them, and on their heart I will write it; and I will be their God, and they shall be My people'" (Jeremiah 31:33).

Among all of the riches included in the gift of divine grace, and one that I oftentimes struggle to live by, is in accepting the fact that I do not, cannot, or have not anything to contribute toward His unmerited grace. I oftentimes find myself trapped by an old pattern of thinking that I have to *do* something in order to earn God's grace. This idea tricks me into thinking that if I do contribute something toward it, then I feel like I deserve it. However, this could not be further from the truth—in fact, this idea is just plain wrong because it implies that Christ died needlessly.

When I read the words that God spoke to Jeremiah about putting His law within them and on their hearts, it brings to mind this definition of marriage that someone once presented to me: "Marriage is a bonding of two souls by the spirit of love. Together their love brings forth a power that one does not have alone. If the marriage is bound by the written law, then it binds but does not bond; but if it is bound by the law that is written on the tablet of your heart, then it bonds but does not bind. Know that law and you will need no other law."

The Old Testament believers were bound by the written law, and because of it, I can understand why it was so difficult for them to bond with God. The Hebrew word for law is *towrah* and is defined to mean "a body of legal instructions." If I think of this in terms of a marriage, then this tells me that it becomes a marriage that is bound by the written law as opposed to a marriage that is bound by the heart. If I think of it in terms of judicial law, then it becomes a system whereby if one breaks the law, then one must pay the penalty. This I fully understand because I have had to pay some expensive fines for getting caught speeding; and have had imposed upon me the requirement to fulfill part of this law by attending an all-day driver education class. In either case, both are binding, and both depend on following a set of legal directives that produce merited rewards. What I find interesting is that although this law sometimes controls my outer behavior, it has not changed my inner behavior. Although I know the law and feel bound to follow it, I still like to speed.

However, based on the *sole merit* of the stupendous work of the crucifixion, death, and resurrection of Christ, the penalty that the judicial law demands was paid in full, and because of this, New Testament believers are now freed from the law. The words that God spoke to Jeremiah have come to pass, and His law now abides in us. In the Sermon on the Mount, Matthew records the following words of Jesus: "Do not think that I came to abolish the Law or the Prophets; I did not come to abolish, but to fulfill" (5:17).

The best way I know to make a clear distinction between the old merit system of law and the new unmerited system of grace is by the following list that I have compiled:

"Divine Grace is a divine occurrence whereby man is the recipient and not the contributor."

Old Covenant (Law) Versus	New Covenant (Grace)
A merited system.	An unmerited system.
A position or standing under the requirements of the law.	A position of standing under God's grace.
Conditional (based on works); an "if" followed by a "then" is always conditional.	Unconditional (based on faith); based on the work of Christ.
If you do this, then you get that.	Because you now have this, you don't have to do in order to get it.
You do in order to get.	You do in order to give.
Self-righteous based on what you do, and requires fulfillment of the law based on your own merit.	Made righteous in Christ based on what Christ did, therefore completely unmerited.
Yoked to the merit system.	Freed from the merit system.
You had to fulfill the requirements of the law and if you didn't, then you were condemned by the law.	Because Christ fulfilled all of the requirements of the law, you are no longer condemned (Romans 8:1).
Unforgiven until you paid for your sins.	Forgiven (past, present, and future) because Christ paid for your sins.
Circumcision made by hands (Ephesians 2:11).	Circumcision made without hands (Colossians 2:11). This circumcision is a spiritual circumcision. I like to think of it as an inner circumcision of the heart as opposed to an outer circumcision of the flesh.

Old Covenant (Law) Versus	New Covenant (Grace)
Think you deserve it because you do it.	Know you don't deserve it because Christ did it for us.
Old law does not change the inner which produces outer results that do not stem from the heart.	New law changes the inner which produces outer results that stem from the heart.

Dr. Lewis Sperry Chafer wraps this up in a nutshell by making this powerful statement:

> "The solution of the problem is to be found in the fact that the law is a system demanding human merit, while the injunctions addressed to the Christian under grace are unrelated to human merit. Since the child of God is already accepted in the Beloved and stands forever in the merit of Christ, application of the merit system to him is both unreasonable and unscriptural" (*Systematic Theology,* volume 3, p. 240).

JUSTIFICATION

"And the gift is not like that which came through the one who sinned;
for on the one hand the judgment arose from one transgression
resulting in condemnation, but on the other hand the free gift arose
from many transgressions resulting in justification" (Romans 5:16).

I think what I love the most about this particular Scripture is that Paul clearly puts this aspect of God's divine grace into perspective with three little words: "the free gift." What I found to be interesting is that the term *justification* is only mentioned three times in the New Testament, and Paul uses two different Greek words to communicate it. The first one that he uses is *dikaioma*, which can be found in Romans 4. It is profoundly translated to mean "a judicial decree made by God by which He acquits man and declares them free from guilt through the imputed righteousness of Christ, *'who was delivered up because of our transgressions and was raised because of our justification'"* (v. 25).

The second time that Paul uses the term *justification* is found in Romans 5 and he chooses to use the word *dikaiosis*, which means "the act of God declaring men free from guilt and acceptable to Him." He sums it up by saying, "So then as through one transgression there resulted condemnation to all men, even so through one act of righteousness there resulted justification of life to all men" (v. 18).

In either case, both declare the judicial decree that was made that acquits man, declares him free from condemnation and judgment, and presents him righteous before God was done solely by an act of God. Without minimizing the significance and the profoundness of the term *justification*, if I relate it to man then I am then able to comprehend its significance. Let's say that we committed every crime that is known to man and were arrested, charged, and put on trial. Then, after the trial, the jury found us to be guilty on all counts, and the judge sentenced us to death. Then a completely innocent person willingly steps forward on our behalf and says, "Judge, I will pay the penalty for them." And because of this one sole act, the judge accepts the offer, slams the gavel down, acquits us on all counts of the charges, and sets us free. Wouldn't that just shock you? Bear in mind that because of the existence of the legal clause of double jeopardy, we can never be charged for any of these crimes again. Moreover, because of the acquittal, these crimes will never appear on our record.

ADOPTION

"He predestined us to adoption as sons through Jesus Christ to Himself, according to the kind intention of His will, to the praise of the glory of His grace, which He freely bestowed upon us in the Beloved" (Ephesians 1:5–6).

Another feature of the riches of divine grace is divine adoption. In human adoption, an outsider may become a legitimate member of a family through the legal system. Likewise, in divine adoption, because God Himself signed the adoption papers with His own blood, a born-again child of God goes from being an outsider to a fully legitimate child of God. Moreover, this divine act of adoption places us in a new position that makes us eligible to receive all of the benefits and privileges that are afforded to all other legitimate family members in the body of Christ, including the inheritance. The Greek word that Paul uses for adoption is *huiothesia,* which means "the nature and condition of the true disciples in Christ, who by receiving the Spirit of God into their souls become sons of God." In John 3:6, Christ calls this being "born again," which He says is a spiritual birth. Once adopted, *"He seals it in Him with the Holy Spirit of promise who is given as a pledge of our inheritance, with a view to the redemption of God's own possession, to the praise of His glory"* (Ephesians 1:13–14), and then lavishes us with more of the riches of His Grace.

Delivered from the
Power of Darkness

"For He delivered us from the domain of darkness, and transferred us to the kingdom of His beloved Son" (Colossians 1:13).

My mind tends to grasp concepts through visualization. When I first meditated on the concept of being delivered out of the sphere of darkness and immediately transferred into the sphere of light, a *Star Wars* scenario came to mind. I could just see myself in a dark dungeon being held prisoner by some evil force similar to Darth Vader. While the galactic war between the forces of good and evil is being fought outside my prison gate, Skywalker comes to rescue me, and with a blink of an eye I'm spirited away from the galactic sphere of darkness and taken to a magnificent kingdom that sits on the top of a high mountain in the sphere of light. However much of a fantasy this picture paints, it is not far from the truth. In his exposition of Colossians 1:13, Dr. Norman L. Geisler writes:

> "This light is the spiritual sphere to which believers have been transferred from the dominion of darkness (Luke 22:53; Acts 26:18; Eph. 6:12). From this dominion (*exousias*, "power, authority") of darkness (John 3:19–20) believers have been

rescued, delivered. Through Christ they were brought from a rebel kingdom and placed under the sovereignty of their rightful King" *(The Bible Knowledge Commentary,* 1983, p. 672).

Additionally, in his careful analysis of this great exchange that Paul writes about in Colossians, Dr. Chafer writes:

"In Colossians 1:13, the term "translated" evidently refers to the removal from the sphere of Satan's dominion to that of Christ. The kingdom is that of God, which may be considered also the kingdom of the Son of His love. Entrance into the kingdom of God is by the new birth (John 3:5). Such a position is far more than merely to be delivered from darkness, however much the advantage of that may be; it is to be inducted into an established in the kingdom of God's dear Son" *(Systematic Theology,* volume 3, p. 248).

In addition to the supernatural acts that simultaneously occur at the time of salvation—of going from a fatherless child to a legitimate son of God; being forgiven for all transgressions past, present and future; being reconciled; being justified; being adopted; being immediately transferred out of the domain of darkness and permanently placed in His kingdom—another stupendous supernatural feature of divine grace is that God makes us legal citizens of heaven.

DIRECT ACCESS TO GOD THE FATHER

"Let us therefore draw near with confidence to the throne of grace,
that we may receive mercy and may find grace in time of need"
(Hebrews 4: 16).

Of all of the features of the riches of divine grace, because of the completed work of Christ, believers now have direct access to God the Father. In the Old Testament, this amazingly high privilege was only given to a handful of believers. Among the most notable were the prophets Abraham and Moses; otherwise, the designated high priests were the only ones who were allowed to enter into the holy of holies to act as mediators on behalf of God's people.

Without deviating too far off of the subject of the riches of divine grace, I thought I would give a little background about what the significance of this particular feature of divine grace is and the supernatural act that occurred when Christ died on the cross.

The Hebrew word for tabernacle is *mishkan* and is defined to mean "dwelling place." The painstaking instructions that were given to Moses for the construction of the tabernacle and the immense dimensions of the curtain that divided the inner portion from the outer portion of the sanctuary, as well as the exact instructions and dimensions for the construction of the veil that separated the inner holy of holies from the holy place inside the sanctuary, are written in detail in Exodus 26–27. "And let them construct a sanctuary for Me, that I may dwell among them. According to all that I am going to show you, as the pattern of the tabernacle and the pattern of all its furniture, just so you shall construct it" (Exodus 25:8–9). This inner "holy of holies" inside the sanctuary is where the mercy seat was placed on the ark of the testimony behind the veil; "and the veil shall serve for you as a partition between the holy place and the holy of holies" (Exodus 26:34).

The writer of Hebrews also writes about some of the details that pertain to the holy of holies. He writes, "Above the ark of the covenant were the cherubim of glory overshadowing the mercy seat" (9:5). What is so significant about all of this is that the great historian Luke records the supernatural act that occurred in the tabernacle when Christ died on the cross. He writes, "And it was now about the sixth hour, and darkness fell over the whole land until the ninth hour, the sun being obscured; and the veil of the temple was torn in two" (Luke 23:44–45).

This short explanation in Eerdman's *International Standard Bible Encyclopedia* gives us a clearer understanding of the importance of understanding the relationship between the tabernacle of the Old Testament and of this particular feature of divine grace that affords direct access to God in the New Testament.

> "It is in the Epistle to the Hebrews that most clearly develops the relation between the tabernacle of the old dispensation and the 'great salvation' of the new. The author emphasizes the divinely ordained but imperfect role that the tabernacle and its services played. The tabernacle was but a copy of the heavenly sanctuary (Heb. 8:5; 9:24; Acts 7:44; Rev: 15:5) and was designed to foreshadow things to come (10:1). Its regulations were temporary (9:10), its sacrifices imperfect (9:9; 10:1–4), and the access it afforded to the divine presence very limited (9:7). But

Christ has offered Himself as a perfect, once-for-all sacrifice (9:12–14, 26). He has entered the heavenly sanctuary not made with human hands (8:2; 9:11), thereby opening a 'new and living way' into God's presence for all believers (10:19–22; 6:19). Believers can therefore approach the 'throne of grace' (i.e., the heavenly counterpart of the tabernacle 'mercy seat' with the confidence that they will obtain the mercy and grace that they need" (4:16). (Eerdman's *International Standard Bible Encyclopedia*, Volume Q-Z, 1979, p. 705, ed. Geoffrey W. Bromiley).

By this stupendous supernatural act, God grants us fellowship with both Him and with His Son. As John so succinctly put it, "What we have seen and heard we proclaim to you also, that you also may have fellowship with us; and indeed our fellowship is with the Father, and with His Son Jesus Christ" (1 John 1:3).

HEAVENLY CITIZENS

"For our citizenship is in heaven, from which also we eagerly wait for a Savior, the Lord Jesus Christ" (Philippians 3:20).

Like in the human realm whereby one is automatically deemed to be a legal citizen of one's country of birth, in the spiritual realm one is also deemed a legal citizen of heaven by *spiritual* birth. Christ clarified this point to Nichodemus in John 3: "Truly, truly, I say to you, unless one is born of water and the Spirit, he cannot enter into the kingdom of God. That which is born of the flesh is flesh; and that which is born of the Spirit is spirit" (vv. 5–6). With few words, Dr. Edwin A. Blum explains what being born of the water means. He writes:

> "There are two distinct realms: one is of fallen man (the flesh) and the other is of God (the Spirit). A fallen person cannot regenerate himself; he needs a divine operation. Only God's Holy Spirit can regenerate a human spirit" *(The Bible Knowledge Commentary,* 1983, p. 281).

Paul was keenly aware of this feature of divine grace. In writing to the Philippians, Paul encourages them to remember that while they are being enculturated by earthly social norms and mores, they were not to set their minds on them, but rather to set their minds on the spiritual truth that their citizenship is in heaven (Philippians 3:19–20). Of this same feature, Dr. Chafer adds the following:

> "Citizenship itself—whether realized at the present moment or not—is an abiding position accorded to all who believe. In truth, the occupation of that citizenship by instant removal from this sphere would be the normal experience for each Christian when he is saved" *(Systematic Theology,* volume 3, p. 252).

I muse over the terms that Peter uses for this new position that divine grace puts us in—he calls believers "aliens and strangers" (1 Peter 2:11). I like to think of it in terms of being "strangers in a strange land" because it reminds me of the time that I lived in a foreign country. Although I adopted the social norms and mores of the new country, the fact that my legal citizenship remained in the country of my birth was always at the forefront of my mind.

Of the many characteristics under the umbrella of this feature of divine grace, one of them is that by the divine act of adoption as sons and daughters through the blood of Christ, we are instantly placed in the household of God. Like the relationship that is established between the members of an earthly family who come from the same bloodline, when believers are born by the spirit an instant relationship is also established between the members of God's family by the blood of Christ. We then suddenly discover that we have spiritual sisters and brothers throughout the world. Paul wrote this to the Ephesians: "So then you are no longer strangers and aliens, but you are fellow-citizens with the saints and are of God's household" (Ephesians 2:19). Understanding this position also helped me to understand that both the phenomenon of sibling rivalry and the squabbles that are often found to exist among members of an earthly family are also found to exist among members of God's spiritual family. Luke makes mention of this occurring between the apostles while being in the full presence of Christ. "And an argument arose among them as to which of them might be the greatest" (Luke 9:46). What I love is the way Christ settled it. He said to them: "For who is least among you, this is the one who is great" (v. 48).

The Inheritance

"I pray that the eyes of your heart may be enlightened, so that you may know what is the hope of His calling, what are the riches of the glory of His inheritance in the saints" (Ephesians 1:18).

Of all of the riches in divine grace, to me, one of the richest is divine inheritance. When I think of an "inheritance," my mind immediately connects it with some earthly estate that is legally left to me by someone which is usually received after the person passes away. If I replace the phrase *earthly estate* with *heavenly estate*, then I get a glimpse of what Peter and Paul mean when they write about the inheritance that Christ procured for us by His work on the cross. Bearing in mind that one is deemed to be a "legal" citizen of heaven by spiritual birth, and sons and daughters of the family in the household of God, then it stands to follow that as heirs and heiresses the divine inheritance would also be legally received after the earthly death. The Greek words for inheritance are *kleronomeo* and *kleronomia* and are translated to mean, "to receive a part of an inheritance; obtain by right of inheritance"; and "what is given to one as a possession; the share which an individual will have in that eternal blessedness," respectively. In trying to comprehend this spiritual truth and uncover the richer meaning behind it, I began by trying to understand the meaning of the term. I found this short explanation in Eerdman's *International Standard Bible Encyclopedia* to be quite helpful.

> "In the New Testament inheritance as the ordinary transmission of property from father to son is found in the parables of Jesus (Mat. 21:38; Mk. 12:1–8; Lk. 15:11–13; 20:14). In these instances sonship is firmly linked with inheritance, reflecting the common Greek and Oriental view. But the New Testament also uses the verb *Kleronomeo* and noun *Kleronomia* in a theological sense as an eschatological concept. In such cases these terms refer to the kingdom of God (see Lk. 10:25; 18:18) as the inheritance now to be claimed by the heirs, the sons of God (Mt. 19:29; 25:34; Mk. 10:17; 1 Cor. 6:9ff.). This sonship is based "not … on physical descent … but on the divine call and appointment." (Eerdman's *International Standard Bible Encyclopedia,* Volume E-J, 1979, p. 824, ed. Geoffrey W. Bromiley).

In the opening chapter of 1 Peter, he reveals his knowledge of the future inheritance by stating this: "Blessed be the God and Father of our Lord Jesus Christ, who according to His great mercy has caused us to be born again to a living hope through the resurrection of Jesus Christ from the dead, to obtain an inheritance which is imperishable and undefiled and will not fade away, *reserved in heaven for you,"* (vv. 3–4). Then, in his opening letter to the Ephesians, Paul describes who and how the guarantee is given. He writes, "In Him, you also, after listening to the message of the truth, the gospel of your salvation—having also believed, you were sealed in Him with the Holy Spirit of promise, who is given as a pledge of our inheritance" (vv. 13–14 a, b). This excerpt from the *Discovering the Believer's Inheritance in Ephesians,* by Ray C. Stedman, helps to visualize how the seal preserves the believer.

"Just as the seal on a letter preserved it from tampering, the Spirit's presence speaks of God's preserving seal upon our lives" (Our Riches in Christ: Discovering the Believer's Inheritance in Ephesians, by Ray C. Stedman, http://www.raystedman.org/ephesians/richesinchrist.html#anchor18617).

Ray Stedman then goes on further to explain this concept:

"The *New International* Version brings out this concept with clarity in rendering Paul's concept of the Holy Spirit as "a deposit guaranteeing our inheritance." In Greek, the word *deposit* is *arrhabon*, which means "a down payment." If you've ever bought a car, you know what *arrhabon* is all about. You sign a paper and pay a down payment, a deposit, and that is the *arrhabon*, the guarantee that there is more to come. The presence of the Spirit in your life—the joy and the peace He gives—is the guarantee that there is more yet to come from God. The Spirit is the down payment on a much greater, fuller, richer experience of God than you have ever known before. The Holy Spirit is just the beginning of the blessings you will receive in Christ."

And, in his exposition of Ephesians, Dr. Harold W. Hoehner writes this:

"The Holy Spirit who seals is a deposit guaranteeing our inheritance. The 'deposit' is more than a pledge which could be returned; it is a down payment with a guarantee of more to come (cf. "the firstfruits of the Spirit," Rom. 8.23). 'A deposit guaranteeing' translates the Greek *arrhabon* (used elsewhere in the New Testament only in 2 Cor. 1:22; 5:5). It guarantees believers' 'inheritance' of salvation and heaven (cf. 1 Peter 1:4). In essence, the 'deposit' of the Holy Spirit is a little bit of heaven in believers' lives with a guarantee of much more yet to come" *(The Bible Knowledge Commentary,* 1983, p. 619).

To compliment these words of Dr. Hoehner, in chapter 2 of Ephesians, Paul further states, "In order that in the ages to come, He might show the surpassing riches of His grace in kindness toward us in Christ Jesus" (Ephesians 2:7).

But what are these "firstfruits" that Paul mentions in Romans chapter 8? Dr. Chafer lists them as follows:

> "These present ministries of the Spirit are said to be an 'earnest" (2 Cor. 1:22; Eph. 1:14) and 'firstfruits' (Rom. 8:23) of the Spirit. There are five of these present riches: (1) The believer is *born* of the Spirit (John 3:6), by which operation Christ is begotten in the one who exercises saving faith. (2) The believer is *baptized* by the Spirit (1 Cor. 12:13), which is a work of the Holy Spirit by which the believer is joined to Christ's Body and comes to be in Christ, and therefore a partaker of all that Christ is. (3) The believer is *indwelt* or *anointed* by the Spirit (John 7:39; Rom. 5:5; 8:9; 2 Cor. 1:21; Gal. 4:6; 1 John 2:27; 3:24) by which Presence the believer is equipped for every conflict and service. (4) The believer is *sealed* by the Spirit (2) Cor. 1:22; Eph. 4:30), which is the work of God the Holy Spirit by which the children of God are made secure unto the day of redemption. (5) The believer may be *filled* with the Spirit (Eph. 5:18), which ministry of the Spirit releases His power and effectiveness in the heart in which He dwells" *(Systematic Theology,* volume 3, p. 264).

But wait—there's more. Paul reveals that this inheritance is twofold. In 1:14 he not only writes about "our" inheritance, but at end of verse 18 he specifically uses the words "His inheritance in the saints," which tells me that Christ has also obtained a legal inheritance. Believers as sons and daughters of God legally obtain the inheritance procured by the death of Christ, and Christ as Son of God legally obtains His inheritance in the saints who are given to Him by His Father. Now I understand what Paul meant when he wrote. "And if children, heirs also, heirs of God and fellow-heirs with Christ" (Romans 8:17a).

A True Sense of Belonging and Security

I grew up with the philosophy that "there is no such thing as security"; and with "the only thing you can really count on in this life is change." As a result, I went through life feeling quite insecure about everything, including believing that the promises that were made to me by those people in my life were all subject to change. In order to find some solid ground on which I could stand, I finally adopted the position of "there is no such thing as security." However, after studying the prayer that Christ prayed to His Father in John 17, and understanding that believers are "His inheritance," these philosophies were all replaced with a new immutable sense of belonging and security.

Beginning with the seven days of creation in Genesis and ending with the seven last plagues mentioned in Revelation 21:9, Scripture is saturated with the number seven. It is to be noted that in Jesus' prayer to His Father, He asks Him to "keep all of those whom His Father has given to Him," and He does this seven times.

In Hebrew, the word *seven* is *shaba* and is translated by Brown, Driver, Briggs, and Gesenius to mean "to swear, take an oath; to swear (of Jehovah by Himself)." Added to this, Strong's translation of *shaba* is defined as "a primitive root; properly to *be complete*, but used only as a denominative; to *seven* oneself, that is, *swear* (as if by repeating a declaration seven times): - adjure, charge (by an oath, with an oath), take an oath."

Based on this revelation, the fact that Jesus prayed to keep all of those whom His Father has given to Him seven times, He is in fact making a powerful declaration of an immutable oath taken between Father and Son.

The first time that Christ uses the phrase "all whom Thou hast given Me" in His prayer in John 17 is in verse 2. Beginning here, Christ asks the Father to give "all of those whom the Father has given to Him, He may give them Eternal life."

The second is found in verse 6b: "I manifested Thy name to the men whom Thou gavest Me out of the world."

The third is found in verse 6c: "Thine they were, and Thou gavest them to Me, and they have kept Thy word."

The fourth is found in verse 9: "I ask on their behalf; I do not ask on behalf of the world, but of those whom Thou hast given Me; for they are Thine."

The fifth is found in verse 11c: "Holy Father, keep them in Thy name, the name which Thou hast given Me; that they may be one, even as We are."

The sixth is found in verse 12: "While I was with them, I was keeping them in Thy name which Thou hast given Me; and I guarded them, and not one of them perished but the son of perdition, that the Scripture might be fulfilled."

And the seventh and final is found in verse 24: "Father, I desire that they also, whom Thou has given Me, be with Me where I am, in order that they may behold My glory, which Thou hast given Me; for Thou didn't love Me before the foundation of the world."

With regard to being "His inheritance," Dr. Chafer writes the following:

"Each Christian is a gift of the Father to the Son; however, beyond the treasure which he is to Christ as a gift from the Father, Ephesians 1:18 asserts that the believer is also the inheritance of the Father. Much is promised the believer respecting his future place in glory. It is written: 'And the glory which thou gavest me I have given them; that they may be one, even as we are one'" (John 17:22); (ibid, p. 261).

And of this same exalted position, Dr. Scofield in his Bible commentary writes this:

"Seven times Jesus speaks of believers as given to Him by the Father (vs. 2, 6 twice, 9, 11, 12, 24). Jesus Christ is God's love-gift to the world (John 3:16), and believers are the Father's love-gift to Jesus Christ. It is Christ who commits the believer to the Father for safe-keeping, so that the believer's security rests upon the Father's faithfulness to His Son Jesus Christ." (John 17, p. 1139)

What is important to keep in mind is that because of the oath taken between God and Christ, all that He asked for on our behalf has been done. This is our true sense of belonging and of security. Personally, I like to think in terms of it being a done deal—signed, sealed, and delivered by the God Most High as an oath to His Son. This sheds a whole new light on the meaning of the powerful statement that Christ made in the previous chapter of John. It also happens to be the one that changed my entire prayer life: "At that day ye shall ask me nothing. Verily, verily, I say unto you, whatsoever ye shall ask the Father in my name, He will give it you" (John 16:23). Christ also repeats this twice in John 14. He states, "And whatever you ask in My name, that will I do, that the Father may be glorified in the Son. If you ask me anything in My name, I will do it" (vv. 14–15).

More Gifts

"If you then, being evil, know how to give good gifts to your children, how much more shall your heavenly Father give the Holy Spirit to those who ask Him?" (Luke 11:13).

When I wrap gifts that I give to others, I sometimes like to collect an array of different ones, wrap them individually and then place them all into one big box. This way, it appears as though it is only one large gift. This is what I think of when I unwrap all of the gifts that are included in the Gift of God's divine grace. I imagine God giving me this beautifully wrapped box, sitting down in front of it, unwrapping it, and finding that it is stuffed with individually wrapped gifts inside. Then, as I open each gift, I become more and more elated by seeing what each one turns out to be.

Included in the box containing individually wrapped gifts, God, Christ, and His Holy Spirit each graciously wrapped their individual gifts and included them in the same package. Paul was keenly aware of this. In writing to the believers in Corinth, Rome, and Ephesus, he insightfully reveals the gifts that are given to the believers by each of the persons of the trinity, and explains the purpose for which they are given.

Beginning with God the Father, in Romans 12, Paul reveals the gifts given by God. "For through the grace given to me I say to every man among you not to think more highly of himself than he ought to think; but to think so as to have sound judgment, as *God* has allotted to each a measure of faith" (v. 3). "And since we have gifts that differ according to the grace given to us, let each one exercise them accordingly: If prophecy, according to the proportion of his faith; if service, in his service; or he who teaches, in his teaching; or he who exhorts, in his exhortation; he who gives with liberality; he who leads, with diligence; he who shows mercy with cheerfulness" (vv. 6–8).

While writing to the Ephesians, in chapter 4 he states, "But to each one of us grace was given according to the measure of *Christ's* gift" (v. 7). "And He gave some as apostles, and some as prophets, and some as evangelists, and some as pastors and teachers" (vv. 11–12).

Finally, while writing to the Corinthians, in chapter 12 of 1 Corinthians, he begins by clarifying the gifts. "Now there are varieties of gifts, but the same *Spirit*, And there are varieties of ministries, and the same *Lord*. And there are varieties of effects, but the same *God* who works all things in all *persons*" (vv. 4–6). "For to one is given the word of wisdom through the Spirit, and to another the word of knowledge according to the same Spirit; to another faith by the same Spirit, and to another gifts of healing by the one Spirit, and to another the effecting of miracles, and to another prophecy, and to another the distinguishing of spirits, to another various kinds of tongues, and to another the interpretation of tongues. But one and the same Spirit works all these things, distributing to each one individually just as He wills" (vv. 8–11).

As legal citizens of heaven, and by the act of divine adoption into the household of God, Paul emphasizes the fact that God, not man, is the one who assigns these gifts individually. "But now God has placed the members, each one of them, in the body, just as He desired" (1 Corinthians 12:18). He then reveals that it is God who graciously empowers His sons and daughters to use these gifts for the purpose of serving and helping one another. "And God has appointed in the church first apostles, second prophets, third teachers, then miracles, then gifts of healings, helps, administrations, various kinds of tongues" (1 Corinthians 12:28). What I found interesting to note is that when all of these gifts given by the Trinity that are recorded in Romans 12:6-8; 1 Corinthians 12:8-10, 28; and Ephesians 4:11 are gathered together, you can readily see that they are all given for the purpose of serving one another. In just a few short words, Paul simply states that the empowerment of these gifts is not for the sake of oneself, but for the sake of the family. "So also you, since you are zealous of spiritual gifts, seek to abound for the edification of the church" (1 Corinthians 14:14). As members of the family, all that is left for us to do is to open the box and unwrap the gifts.

"Peace I leave with you; My Peace I give to you; not as the world gives, do I give to you. Let not your heart be troubled, nor let it be fearful" (John 14:27).

"And He is clothed with a robe dipped in blood; and His Name is called The Word of God" (Revelation 19:13).

Epilogue

Because I was taught that it is more blessed to give than to receive, it has been difficult to accept the tremendous amount of riches of "unmerited" divine grace that God lavishes upon us without feeling like I have to contribute something to it. Even after getting a glimpse of the stupendous work that Christ did on our behalf, I still continue to struggle with believing that all He asks for in return is to accept His love, to believe in Him, to have an intimate relationship with Him, and to submit to His kind will for our lives on a daily basis. This is not much different from what an earthly father would want from his own child.

One of my favorite Scriptures about grace is written by Paul. In writing to the Corinthians, he tells them what God personally said to him after he prayed for the removal of the "thorn in his flesh." He writes, "And He has said to me, 'My grace is sufficient for you, for power is perfected in weakness'" (2 Corinthians 12:9). But I say, "His grace is *more* than sufficient for me."

Appendix G
New American Standard
Greek Lexicon

The New Testament Greek lexicon is based on Thayer's and Smith's Bible Dictionary, plus others. It is keyed to Gerhard Kittel's *Theological Dictionary of the New Testament*. These works are in the public domain.

Agapē (Strong's Number 26)
Parts of Speech – Noun Feminine
Phonetic Spelling: *ag-ah'-pay*
Definition

1. brotherly love, affection, good will, love, benevolence
2. love feasts

NAS Word Usage - Total: 116
beloved 1, love 1, love 112, love feasts 1, love's 1

NAS Verse
Matthew 24:12
Luke 11:42
John 5:42; 13:35; 15:9–10; 15:13; 17:26
Romans 5:5; 5:8; 8:35; 8:39; 12:9; 13:10; 14:15; 15:30

1 Corinthians 4:21; 8:1; 13:1–4; 13:8; 13:13; 14:1; 16:14; 16:24
2 Corinthians 2:4; 2:8; 5:14; 6:6; 8:7–8; 8:24; 13:11; 13:14
Galatians 5:6; 5:13; 5:22
Ephesians 1:15; 2:4; 3:17; 3:19; 4:2; 4:15–16; 5:2; 6:23
Philippians 1:9; 1:16; 2:1–2
Colossians 1:4; 1:8; 1:13; 2:2; 3:14
1 Thessalonians 1:3; 3:6; 3:12; 5:8; 5:13
2 Thessalonians 1:3; 2:10; 3:5
1 Timothy 1:5; 1:14; 2:15; 4:12; 6:11
2 Timothy 1:7; 1:13; 2:22; 3:10
Titus 2:2
Philemon 1:5; 1:7; 1:9
Hebrews 6:10; 10:24
1 Peter 4:8; 5:14
2 Peter 1:7
1 John 2:5; 2:15; 3:1; 3:16–17; 4:7–10; 4:12; 4:16–18; 5:3
2 John 1:3; 1:6
3 John 1:6
Jude 1:2; 1:12; 1:21
Revelation 2:4; 2:19

Agapaō (Strong's Number 25)
Parts of Speech – Verb
Phonetic Spelling: *ag-ap-ah'o*
Definition

1. of persons
   a. to welcome, to entertain, to be fond of, to love dearly
2. of things
   a. to be well pleased, to be contented at or with a thing

NAS Word Usage - Total: 143
beloved 8, felt a love for 1, love 1, love 75, loved 38, loves 20

NAS Verse
Matthew 5:43–44; 5:46; 6:24; 19:19; 22:37; 22:39

Mark 10:21; 12:30–31; 12:33
Luke 6:27; 6:32; 6:35; 7:5; 7:42; 7:47; 10:27; 11:43; 16:13
John 3:16; 3:19; 3:35; 8:42; 10:17; 11:5; 12:43; 13:1; 13:23; 13:34;
     14:15; 14:21; 14:23–24; 14:28; 14:31; 15:9; 15:12; 15:17;
     17:23–24; 17:26; 19:26; 21:7; 21:15–16; 21:20
Romans 8:28; 8:37; 9:13; 9:25; 13:8–9
1 Corinthians 8:3
2 Corinthians 9:7; 11:11; 12:15
Galatians 2:20; 5:14
Ephesians 1:6; 2:4; 5:2; 5:25; 5:28; 5:33; 6:24
Colossians 3:12; 3:19
1 Thessalonians 1:4; 4:9
2 Thessalonians 2:13; 2:16
2 Timothy 4:8; 4:10
Hebrews 1:9; 12:6
James 1:12; 2:5; 2:8
1 Peter 1:8; 1:22; 2:17; 3:10
2 Peter 2:15
1 John 2:10; 2:15; 3:10–11; 3:14; 3:18; 3:23; 4:7–8; 4:10–12;
     4:19–21; 5:1–2
2 John 1:1; 1:5
3 John 1:1
Jude 1:1
Revelation 1:5; 3:9; 12:11; 20:9

Aiōn (Strong's Number 165)
Parts of Speech – Noun Masculine
Phonetic Spelling: *ahee-ohn'*
Definition

   1. forever, an unbroken age, perpetuity of time, eternity
   2. the worlds, universe
   3. period of time, age

NAS Word Usage - Total: 95
age 20, ages 6, ancient time 1, beginning of time 1, course 1, eternal 2,

eternity 1, ever 2, forever 27, forever and ever 20, forevermore 2, long ago 1, never* 1, old 1, time 1, world 7, worlds 1

NAS Verse
Matthew 6:13; 12:32; 13:22; 13:39–40; 13:49; 21:19; 24:3; 28:20
Mark 3:29; 4:19; 10:30; 11:14
Luke 1:33; 1:55; 1:70; 16:8; 18:30; 20:34–35
John 6:51; 6:58; 8:35; 9:32; 12:34; 14:16
Acts 3:21; 15:18
Romans 1:25; 9:5; 11:36; 12:2; 16:27
1 Corinthians 1:20; 2:6–8; 3:18; 10:11
2 Corinthians 4:4; 9:9; 11:31
Galatians 1:4–5
Ephesians 1:21; 2:2; 2:7; 3:9; 3:11; 3:21
Philippians 4:20
Colossians 1:26
1 Timothy 1:17; 6:17
2 Timothy 4:10; 4:18
Titus 2:12
Hebrews 1:2; 1:8; 5:6; 6:5; 6:20; 7:17; 7:21; 7:24; 7:28; 9:26; 11:3; 13:8; 13:21
1 Peter 1:25; 4:11; 5:11
2 Peter 3:18
1 John 2:17
2 John 1:2
Jude 1:13; 1:25
Revelation 1:6; 1:18; 4:9–10; 5:13; 7:12; 10:6; 11:15; 14:11; 15:7; 19:3; 20:10; 22:5

Aphesis (Strong's Number 859)
Parts of Speech – Noun Feminine
Phonetic Spelling: *af'-es-is*
Definition

1. release from bondage or imprisonment

2. forgiveness or pardon, of sins (letting them go as if they had never been committed), remission of the penalty

NAS Word Usage - Total: 17
forgiveness 15, free* 1, release 1

NAS Verse
Matthew 26:28
Mark 1:4; 3:29
Luke 1:77; 3:3; 4:18; 24:47
Acts 2:38; 5:31; 10:43; 13:38; 26:18
Ephesians 1:7
Colossians 1:14
Hebrews 9:22; 10:18

Aphiēmi (Strong's Number 863)
Parts of Speech – Verb
Phonetic Spelling: *af-ee'-ay-mee*
Definition

1. to *send forth*, in various applications: cry, forgive, forsake, lay aside, leave, let (alone, be, go, have), omit, put (send) away, remit, suffer, yield up.
2. to send away
   a. to bid going away or depart
      1. of a husband divorcing his wife
   b. to send forth, yield up, to expire
   c. to let go, let alone, let be
      1. to disregard
      2. to leave, not to discuss now, (a topic) 1c
3. of teachers, writers and speakers
      1. to omit, neglect
   a. to let go, give up a debt, forgive, to remit
   b. to give up, keep no longer
4. to permit, allow, not to hinder, to give up a thing to a person
   a. to leave, go away from one in order to go to another place

b. to depart from any one
c. to depart from one and leave him to himself so that all mutual claims are abandoned
d. to desert wrongfully
e. to go away leaving something behind
f. to leave one by not taking him as a companion
g. to leave on dying, leave behind one
h. to leave so that what is left may remain, leave remaining
i. abandon, leave destitute

NAS Word Usage - Total: 146

abandoned 1, allow 5, allowed 2, divorce 2, forgave 2, forgive 23, forgiven 23, forgives 1, gave ... permission 1, leave 7, leaves 2, leaving 8, left 38, let 9, let ... alone 6, let him have 1, neglected 1, neglecting 2, permit 6, permitted 1, permitting 1, send ... away 1, tolerate 1, uttered 1, yielded 1

NAS Verse

Matthew 3:15; 4:11; 4:20; 4:22; 5:24; 5:40; 6:12; 6:14–15; 7:4; 8:15; 8:22; 9:2; 9:5–6; 12:31–32; 13:30; 13:36; 15:14; 18:12; 18:21; 18:27; 18:32; 18:35; 19:14; 19:27; 19:29; 22:22; 22:25; 23:13; 23:23; 23:38; 24:2; 24:40–41; 26:44; 26:56; 27:49–50

Mark 1:18; 1:20; 1:31; 1:34; 2:5; 2:7; 2:9–10; 3:28; 4:12; 4:36; 5:19; 5:37; 7:8; 7:12; 7:27; 8:13; 10:14; 10:28–29; 11:6; 11:16; 11:25–26; 12:12; 12:19–20; 12:22; 13:2; 13:34; 14:6; 14:50; 15:36–37

Luke 4:39; 5:11; 5:20–21; 5:23–24; 6:42; 7:47–49; 8:51; 9:60; 10:30; 11:4; 12:10; 12:39; 13:8; 13:35; 17:3–4; 17:34–36; 18:16; 18:28–29; 19:44; 21:6; 23:34

John 4:3; 4:28; 4:52; 8:29; 10:12; 11:44; 11:48; 12:7; 14:18; 14:27; 16:28; 16:32; 18:8; 20:23

Acts 5:38; 8:22; 14:17

Romans 1:27; 4:7

1 Corinthians 7:11–13

Hebrews 2:8; 6:1

James 5:15
1 John 1:9; 2:12
Revelation 2:4; 2:20; 11:9

Arrhabōn (Strong's Number 728)
Parts of Speech – Noun Masculine
Phonetic Spelling: *ar-hrab-ohn'*
Definition

an earnest

    a.   money which in purchases is given as a pledge or down
        payment that the full amount will subsequently be paid

NAS Word Usage - Total: 3
Given as a pledge 1, pledge 2

NAS Verse
2 Corinthians 1:22; 5:5
Ephesians 1:14

Charis (Strong's Number 5485)
Parts of Speech – Noun Feminine
Phonetic Spelling: *khar'-ece*
Definition

    1. grace
        a. that which affords joy, pleasure, delight, sweetness,
            charm, loveliness: grace of speech
    2. good will, loving kindness, favor
        a. of the merciful kindness by which God, exerting
            his holy influence upon souls, turns them to Christ,
            keeps, strengthens, increases them in Christian faith,
            knowledge, affection, and kindles them to the exercise
            of the Christian virtues

3. what is due to grace
   a. the spiritual condition of one governed by the power of divine grace
   b. the token or proof of grace, benefit
      1. a gift of grace
      2. benefit, bounty
4. thanks (for benefits, services, favors), recompense, reward

NAS Word Usage - Total: 156
blessing 1, concession 1, credit 3, favor 11, gift 1, grace 122, gracious 2, gracious work 3, gratitude 1, thank 3, thankfulness 2, thanks 6

NAS Verse
Luke 1:30; 2:40; 2:52; 4:22; 6:32–34; 17:9
John 1:14; 1:16–17
Acts 2:47; 4:33; 6:8; 7:10; 7:46; 11:23; 13:43; 14:3; 14:26; 15:11; 15:40; 18:27; 20:24; 20:32; 24:27; 25:3; 25:9
Romans 1:5; 1:7; 3:24; 4:4; 4:16; 5:2; 5:15; 5:17; 5:20–21; 6:1; 6:14–15; 6:17; 7:25; 11:5–6; 12:3; 12:6; 15:15; 16:20; 16:24
1 Corinthians 1:3–4; 3:10; 10:30; 15:10; 15:57; 16:3; 16:23
2 Corinthians 1:2; 1:12; 1:15; 2:14; 4:15; 6:1; 8:1; 8:4; 8:6–7; 8:9; 8:16; 8:19; 9:8; 9:14–15; 12:9; 13:14
Galatians 1:3; 1:6; 1:15; 2:9; 2:21; 5:4; 6:18
Ephesians 1:2; 1:6; 2:5; 2:7–8; 3:2; 3:7–8; 4:7; 4:29; 6:24
Philippians 1:2; 1:7; 4:23
Colossians 1:2; 1:6; 3:16; 4:6; 4:18
1 Thessalonians 1:1; 5:28
2 Thessalonians 1:2; 1:12; 2:16; 3:18
1 Timothy 1:2; 1:12; 1:14; 6:21
2 Timothy 1:2–3; 1:9; 2:1; 4:22
Titus 1:4; 2:11; 3:7; 3:15
Philemon 1:3; 1:25
Hebrews 2:9; 4:16; 10:29; 12:15; 12:28; 13:9; 13:25
James 4:6
1 Peter 1:2; 1:10; 1:13; 2:19–20; 3:7; 4:10; 5:5; 5:10; 5:12
2 Peter 1:2; 3:18

2 John 1:3
Jude 1:4
Revelation 1:4; 22:21

Dikaiōma (Strong's Number 1345)
Parts of Speech – Noun Neuter
Phonetic Spelling: *dik-ah'-yo-mah*
Definition

1. that which has been deemed right so as to have force of
   law
   a. what has been established, and ordained by law, an
      ordinance
   b. a judicial decision, sentence
      1. of God 1b
   c. either the favorable judgment by which he acquits
      man and declares them acceptable to Him 1b
   d. unfavorable: sentence of condemnation
2. a righteous act or deed

NAS Word Usage - Total: 10
act of righteousness 1, justification 1, ordinance 1, regulations 2,
requirement 1, requirements 2, righteous acts 2

NAS Verse
Luke 1:6
Romans 1:32; 2:26; 5:16; 5:18; 8:4
Hebrews 9:1; 9:10
Revelation 15:4; 19:8

Dikaiōsis (Strong's Number 1347)
Parts of Speech – Noun Feminine
Phonetic Spelling: *dik-ah'-yo-sis*
Definition

1. the act of God declaring men free from guilt and acceptable to Him
2. abjuring to be righteous, justification

NAS Word Usage - Total: 2
justification 2
NAS Verse
Romans 4:25; 5:18

Eklektos (Strong's Number 1588)
Parts of Speech – Adjective
Phonetic Spelling: *ek-lek-tos'*
Definition

picked out, chosen

a. chosen by God,
    1. to obtain salvation through Christ 1a
b. Christians are called "chosen or elect" of God
    1. the Messiah in called "elect," as appointed by God to the most exalted office conceivable
    2. choice, select, i.e. the best of its kind or class, excellence preeminent: applied to certain individual Christians

NAS Word Usage - Total: 22
choice 2, choice man 1, chosen 1, chosen 9, chosen one 1, elect 8

NAS Verse
Matthew 22:14; 24:22; 24:24; 24:31
Mark 13:20; 13:22; 13:27
Luke 18:7; 23:35
Romans 8:33; 16:13
Colossians 3:12
1 Timothy 5:21
2 Timothy 2:10

Titus 1:1
1 Peter 2:4; 2:6; 2:9
2 John 1:1; 1:13
Revelation 17:14

Euaggelizō (Strong's Number 2097)
Parts of Speech – Verb
Phonetic Spelling: *yoo-ang-ghel-id'-zo*
Definition

1. to bring good news, to announce glad tidings
   a. used in the Old Testament of any kind of good news
      1. of the joyful tidings of God's kindness, in particular, of the Messianic blessings
   b. in the New Testament used especially of the glad tidings of the coming kingdom of God, and of the salvation to be obtained in it through Christ, and of what relates to this salvation
   c. glad tidings are brought to one, one has glad tidings proclaimed to him
   d. to proclaim glad tidings
      1. instruct (men) concerning the things that pertain to Christian salvation

NAS Word Usage - Total: 61
Bring ... good news 2, bring good news 1, brought ... good news 1, good news 5, good news preached 2, gospel 2, gospel preached 2, preach 4, preach the gospel 11, preach ... a gospel 1, preach ... the good news 1, preached 11, preached the gospel 4, preaching 8, preaching the good news 1, preaching the gospel 4, preaching ... a gospel 1

NAS Verse
Matthew 11:5
Luke 1:19; 2:10; 3:18; 4:18; 4:43; 7:22; 8:1; 9:6; 16:16; 20:1

Acts 5:42; 8:4; 8:12; 8:25; 8:35; 8:40; 10:36; 11:20; 13:32; 14:7;
    14:15; 14:21; 15:35; 16:10; 17:18
Romans 1:15; 10:15; 15:20
1 Corinthians 1:17; 9:16; 9:18; 15:1–2
2 Corinthians 10:16; 11:7
Galatians 1:8–9; 1:11; 1:16; 1:23; 4:13
Ephesians 2:17; 3:8
1 Thessalonians 3:6
Hebrews 4:2; 4:6
1 Peter 1:12; 1:25; 4:6
Revelation 10:7; 14:6

Euaggelion (Strong's Number 2098)
Parts of Speech – Noun Neuter
Phonetic Spelling: yoo-ang-ghel'-ee-on
Definition

1. a reward for good tidings
2. good tidings
   a. The glad tidings of the kingdom of God soon to be
      set up, and subsequently also of Jesus the Messiah, the
      founder of this kingdom. After the death of Christ,
      the term comprises also the preaching of (concerning)
      Jesus Christ as having suffered death on the cross to
      procure eternal salvation for the men in the kingdom
      of God, but as restored to life and exalted to the right
      hand of God in heaven, thence to return in majesty to
      consummate the kingdom of God
   b. the glad tidings of salvation through Christ
   c. the proclamation of the grace of God manifest and
      pledged in Christ
   d. the gospel
   e. as the messianic rank of Jesus was proved by his
      words, his deeds, and his death, the narrative of the
      sayings, deeds, and death of Jesus Christ came to be
      called the gospel or glad tidings

NAS Word Usage - Total: 76
good news 1, gospel 73, gospel's 2

NAS Verse
Matthew 4:23; 9:35; 24:14; 26:13
Mark 1:1; 1:14–15; 8:35; 10:29; 13:10; 14:9; 16:15
Acts 15:7; Acts 20:24
Romans 1:1; 1:9; 1:16; 2:16; 10:16; 11:28; 15:16; 15:19; 16:25
1 Corinthians 4:15; 9:12; 9:14; 9:18; 9:23; 15:1
2 Corinthians 2:12; 4:3–4; 8:18; 9:13; 10:14; 11:4; 11:7
Galatians 1:6–7; 1:11; 2:2; 2:5; 2:7; 2:14
Ephesians 1:13; 3:6; 6:15; 6:19
Philippians 1:5; 1:7; 1:12; 1:16; 1:27; 2:22; 4:3; 4:15
Colossians 1:23
1 Thessalonians 1:5; 2:2; 2:4; 2:8–9; 3:2
2 Thessalonians 1:8; 2:14
1 Timothy 1:11
2 Timothy 1:8; 1:10; 2:8
Philemon 1:13
1 Peter 4:17
Revelation 14:6

Euprepeia (Strong's Number 2143)
Parts of Speech – Noun Feminine
Phonetic Spelling: yoo-prep'-*i-ah*
Definition

goodly appearance, shapeliness, beauty, comeliness

NAS Word Usage - Total: 1
beauty 1

NAS Verse
James 1:11

Exousia (Strong's Number 1849)
Parts of Speech – Noun Feminine
Phonetic Spelling: *ex-oo-see'-ah*
Definition

1. power of choice, liberty of doing as one pleases
   a. leave or permission
2. physical and mental power
   a. the ability or strength with which one is endued, which he either possesses or exercises
3. the power of authority (influence) and of right (privilege)
4. the power of rule or government (the power of him whose will and commands must be submitted to by others and obeyed)
   a. universally
      1. authority over mankind
   b. specifically
      1. the power of judicial decisions
      2. of authority to manage domestic affairs
   c. metonymically
      1. a thing subject to authority or rule 4c
   d. jurisdiction
      1. one who possesses authority 4c
   e. a ruler, a human magistrate 4c
   f. the leading and more powerful among created beings superior to man, spiritual potentates
   g. a sign of the husband's authority over his wife
      1. the veil with which propriety required a women to cover herself
   h. the sign of regal authority, a crown

NAS Word Usage - Total: 102
authorities 7, authority 65, charge 1, control 1, domain 2, dominion 1, jurisdiction 1, liberty 1, power 11, powers 1, right 11

NAS Verse
Matthew 7:29; 8:9; 9:6; 9:8; 10:1; 21:23–24; 21:27; 28:18
Mark 1:22; 1:27; 2:10; 3:15; 6:7; 11:28–29; 11:33; 13:34
Luke 4:6; 4:32; 4:36; 5:24; 7:8; 9:1; 10:19; 12:5; 12:11; 19:17; 20:2;
    20:8; 20:20; 22:53; 23:7
John 1:12; 5:27; 10:18; 17:2; 19:10–11
Acts 1:7; 5:4; 8:19; 9:14; 26:10; 26:12; 26:18
Romans 9:21; 13:1–3
1 Corinthians 7:37; 8:9; 9:4–6; 9:12; 9:18; 11:10; 15:24
2 Corinthians 10:8; 13:10
Ephesians 1:21; 2:2; 3:10; 6:12
Colossians 1:13; 1:16; 2:10; 2:15
2 Thessalonians 3:9
Titus 3:1
Hebrews 13:10
1 Peter 3:22
Jude 1:25
Revelation 2:26; 6:8; 9:3; 9:10; 9:19; 11:6; 12:10; 13:2; 13:4–5;
    13:7; 13:12; 14:18; 16:9; 17:12–13; 18:1; 20:6; 22:14

Gennaō (Strong's Number 1080)
Parts of Speech – Verb
Phonetic Spelling: *ghen-nah'-o*
Definition
1. of men who fathered children
   a. to be born
   b. to be begotten
      1. of women giving birth to children
2. metaph.
   a. to engender, cause to arise, excite
   b. in a Jewish sense, of one who brings others over to his way of life, to convert someone
   c. of God making Christ his son
   d. of God making men his sons through faith in Christ's work

NAS Word Usage – Total: 96
(bear 1, bearing children 1, became the father of 4, became ...
father 1, begotten 4, bore 1, born 41, Child 1, conceived 1, father 37,
Father 1, gave 1, gives birth 1, produce 1

NAS Verse
Matthew 1:2–16; 1:20; 2:1; 2:4; 19:12; 26:24
Mark 14:21
Luke 1:13; 1:35; 1:57; 23:29
John 1:13; 3:3–8; 8:41; 9:2; 9:19–20; 9:32; 9:34; 16:21; 18:37
Acts 2:8; 7:8; 7:20; 7:29; 13:33; 22:3; 22:28
Romans 9:11
1 Corinthians 4:15
Galatians 4:23–24; 4:29
2 Timothy 2:23
Philemon 1:10
Hebrews 1:5; 5:5; 11:23
2 Peter 2:12
1 John 2:29; 3:9; 4:7; 5:1; 5:4; 5:18

Huiothesia (Strong's Number 5206)
Parts of Speech – Noun Feminine
Phonetic Spelling: *hwee-oth-es-ee'-ah*
Definition

adoption, adoption as sons

  a. that relationship which God was pleased to establish between
      himself and the Israelites in preference to all other nations
  b. the nature and condition of the true disciples in Christ, who by
      receiving the Spirit of God into their souls become sons of God
  c. the blessed state looked for in the future life after the
      visible return of Christ from heaven

NAS Word Usage – Total (5) adoption as sons

NAS Verse
Romans 8:15; 8:23; 9:4
Galatians 4:5
Ephesians 1:5

Kaleō (Strong's Number 2564)
Parts of Speech – Verb
Phonetic Spelling: *kal-eh'-o*
Definition

1. to call
   a. to call aloud, utter in a loud voice
   b. to invite
2. to call, i.e. to name, by name
   a. to give a name to
      1. to receive the name of, receive as a name
      2. to give some name to one, call his name
   b. to be called, i.e. to bear a name or title (among men)
   c. to salute one by name

NAS Word Usage - Total: 147
call 13, called 99, calling 2, calls 7, give 1, invite 2, invited 15, invited guests 1, invites 1, name given 1, named 2, so-called 1, summoned 2

NAS Verse
Matthew 1:21; 1:23; 1:25; 2:7; 2:16; 2:23; 4:21; 5:9; 5:19; 9:13; 20:8; 21:13; 22:3–4; 22:8–9; 22:43; 22:45; 23:7–10; 25:14; 27:8
Mark 1:20; 2:17; 3:31; 11:17
Luke 1:13; 1:32; 1:35–36; 1:59–62; 1:76; 2:4; 2:21; 2:23; 5:32; 6:15; 6:46; 7:11; 7:39; 8:2; 9:10; 10:39; 14:7–10; 14:12–13; 14:16–17; 14:24; 15:19; 15:21; 19:2; 19:13; 19:29; 20:44; 21:37; 22:3; 22: 25; 23:33
John 1:42; 2:2
Acts 1:12; 1:19; 1:23; 3:11; 4:18; 7:58; 8:10; 9:11; 10:1; 13:1; 14:12; 15:22; 15:37; 24:2; 27:8; 27:14; 27:16; 28:1

Romans 4:17; 8:30; 9:7; 9:11; 9:24–26
1 Corinthians 1:9; 7:15; 7:17–18; 7:20–22; 7:24; 10:27; 15:9
Galatians 1:6; 1:15; 5:8; 5:13
Ephesians 4:1; 4:4
Colossians 3:15
1 Thessalonians 2:12; 4:7; 5:24
2 Thessalonians 2:14
1 Timothy 6:12
2 Timothy 1:9
Hebrews 2:11; 3:13; 5:4; 9:15; 11:8; 11:18
James 2:23
1 Peter 1:15; 2:9; 2:21; 3:6; 3:9; 5:10
2 Peter 1:3
1 John 3:1
Revelation 1:9; 11:8; 12:9; 16:16; 19:9; 19:11; 19:13

Katallassō (Strong's Number 2644)
Parts of Speech – Verb
Phonetic Spelling: *kat-al-las'-so*
Definition

1. to change, exchange, as coins for others of equivalent value
   a. to reconcile (those who are at variance)
   b. return to favor with, be reconciled to one
   c. to receive one into favor

NAS Word Usage - Total: 6
reconciled 5, reconciling 1

NAS Verse
Romans 5:10
1 Corinthians 7:11
2 Corinthians 5:18–20

klēronomeō (Strong's Number 2816)
Parts of Speech – Verb
Phonetic Spelling: *klay-ron-om-eh'-o*
Definition

1. to receive a lot, receive by lot
   a. esp. to receive a part of an inheritance, receive as an inheritance, obtain by right of inheritance
   b. to be an heir, to inherit
2. to receive the portion assigned to one, receive an allotted portion, receive as one's own or as a possession
3. to become partaker of, to obtain

NAS Word Usage - Total: 18
heir 1, inherit 16, inherited 1

NAS Verse
Matthew 5:5; 19:29; 25:34
Mark 10:17
Luke 10:25; 18:18
1 Corinthians 6:9–10; 15:50
Galatians 4:30; 5:21
Hebrews 1:4; 1:14; 6:12; 12:17
1 Peter 3:9
Revelation 21:7

klēronomia (Strong's Number 2817)
Parts of Speech – Noun Feminine
Phonetic Spelling: *klay-ron-om-ee'-ah*
Definition

1. an inheritance, property received (or to be received) by inheritance
2. what is given to one as a possession
   a. the eternal blessedness of the consummated kingdom of God which is to be expected after the visible return of Christ

b. the share which an individual will have in that eternal blessedness

NAS Word Usage - Total: 14
inheritance 14

NAS Verse
Matthew 21:38
Mark 12:7
Luke 12:13; 20:14
Acts 7:5; 20:32
Galatians 3:18
Ephesians 1:14; 1:18; 5:5
Colossians 3:24
Hebrews 9:15; 11:8
1 Peter 1:4

Klētos (Strong's Number 2822)
Parts of Speech – Adjective
Phonetic Spelling: *klay-tos'*
Definition

called, invited (to a banquet)

a. invited (by God in the proclamation of the Gospel) to obtain eternal salvation in the kingdom through Christ
b. called to (the discharge of) some office
    1. divinely selected and appointed

NAS Word Usage - Total: 10
called 9, calling 1

NAS Verse
Matthew 22:14
Romans 1:1; 1:6–7; 8:28
1 Corinthians 1:1–2; 1:24

Jude 1:1
Revelation 17:14

Kosmos (Strong's Number 2889)
Parts of Speech – Noun Masculine
Phonetic Spelling: *kos'-mos*
Definition

1. an apt and harmonious arrangement or constitution, order, government
2. ornament, decoration, adornment, i.e. the arrangement of the stars, "the heavenly hosts," as the ornament of the heavens.
3. the world, the universe
4. the circle of the earth, the earth
5. the inhabitants of the earth, men, the human family
6. the ungodly multitude; the whole mass of men alienated from God, and therefore hostile to the cause of Christ
7. world affairs, the aggregate of things earthly
   a. the whole circle of earthly goods, endowments riches, advantages, pleasures, etc, which although hollow and frail and fleeting, stir desire, seduce from God and are obstacles to the cause of Christ
8. any aggregate or general collection of particulars of any sort
   a. the Gentiles as contrasted to the Jews (Rom. 11:12, etc.)
   b. of believers only, John 1:29; 3:16; 3:17; 6:33; 12:47; 1 Cor. 4:9; 2 Cor. 5:19

NAS Word Usage - Total: 186
adornment 1, world 184, world's 1

NAS Verse
Matthew 4:8; 5:14; 13:35; 13:38; 16:26; 18:7; 24:21; 25:34; 26:13
Mark 8:36; 14:9; 16:15
Luke 9:25; 11:50; 12:30
John 1:9–10; 1:29; 3:16–17; 3:19; 4:42; 6:14; 6:33; 6:51; 7:4; 7:7; 8:12; 8:23; 8:26; 9:5; 9:39; 10:36; 11:9; 11:27; 12:19; 12:25;

12:31; 12:46–47; 13:1; 14:17; 14:19; 14:22; 14:27; 14:30–31; 15:18–19; 16:8; 16:11; 16:20–21; 16:28; 16:33; 17:5–6; 17:9; 17:11; 17:13–16; 17:18; 17:21; 17:23–25; 18:20; 18:36–37; 21:25
Acts 17:24
Romans 1:8; 1:20; 3:6; 3:19; 4:13; 5:12–13; 11:12; 11:15
1 Corinthians 1:20–21; 1:27–28; 2:12; 3:19; 3:22; 4:9; 4:13; 5:10; 6:2; 7:31; 7:33–34; 8:4; 11:32; 14:10
2 Corinthians 1:12; 5:19; 7:10
Galatians 4:3; 6:14
Ephesians 1:4; 2:2; 2:12
Philippians 2:15
Colossians 1:6; 2:8; 2:20
1 Timothy 1:15; 3:16; 6:7
Hebrews 4:3; 9:26; 10:5; 11:7; 11:38
James 1:27; 2:5; 3:6; 4:4
1 Peter 1:20; 3:3; 5:9
2 Peter 1:4; 2:5; 2:20; 3:6
1 John 2:2; 2:15–17; 3:1; 3:13; 3:17; 4:1; 4:3–5; 4:9; 4:14; 4:17; 5:4–5; 5:19
2 John 1:7
Revelation 11:15; 13:8; 17:8

Lutroō (Strong's Number 3084)
Parts of Speech – Verb
Phonetic Spelling: loo-tro'-o
Definition

1. to release on receipt of ransom
2. to redeem, liberate by payment of ransom
   a. to liberate
   b. to cause to be released to oneself by payment of a ransom
   c. to redeem
   d. to deliver from evils of every kind, internal and external

NAS Word Usage - Total: 3
redeem 2, redeemed 1

NAS Verse
Luke 24:21
Titus 2
1 Peter 1:18

Lutrōsis (Strong's Number 3085)
Parts of Speech – Noun Feminine
Phonetic Spelling: loo'-tro-sis
Definition

1. a ransoming, redemption
2. deliverance, esp. from the penalty of sin

NAS Word Usage - Total: 3
redemption 3

NAS Verse
Luke 1:68; 2:38
Hebrews 9:12

Oikoumenē (Strong's Number 3625)
Parts of Speech – Noun Feminine
Phonetic Spelling: *oy-kou-men'-ay*
Definition

1. the inhabited earth
   a. the portion of the earth inhabited by the Greeks, in distinction from the lands of the barbarians
   b. the Roman empire, all the subjects of the empire
   c. the whole inhabited earth, the world
   d. the inhabitants of the earth, men
2. the universe, the world

NAS Word Usage - Total: 15
inhabited earth 1, world 14

NAS Verse
Matthew 24:14
Luke 2:1; 4:5; 21:26
Acts 11:28; 17:6; 17:31; 19:27; 24:5
Romans 10:18
Hebrews 1:6; 2:5
Revelation 3:10; 12:9; 16:14

Phileō (Strong's Number 5368)
Parts of Speech – Verb
Phonetic Spelling: fil-eh'o
Definition

1. to love
    a. to approve of
    b. to like
    c. sanction
    d. to treat affectionately or kindly, to welcome, befriend
2. to show signs of love
    a. to kiss
3. to be fond of doing
    a. to be wont, use to do

NAS Word Usage - Total: 25
kiss 3, love 13, loved 3, loves 6

NAS Verse
Matthew 6:5; 10:37; 23:6; 26:48
Mark 14:44
Luke 20:46; 22:47
John 5:20; 11:3; 11:36; 12:25; 15:19; 16:27; 20:2; 21:15–17
1 Corinthians 16:22
Titus 3:15

Revelation 3:19; 22:15

Proorizō (Strong's Number 4309)
Parts of Speech – Verb
Phonetic Spelling: pro-or-id'-zo
Definition

1. to predetermine, decide beforehand
2. in the New Testament of God decreeing from eternity
3. to foreordain, appoint beforehand

NAS Word Usage - Total: 6
predestined 6

NAS Verse
Acts 4:28
Romans 8:29–30
1 Corinthians 2:7
Ephesians 1:5; 1:11

Proskaleomai (Strong's Number 4341)
Parts of Speech – Verb
Phonetic Spelling: *pros-kal-eh'-om-ahee*
Definition

1. to call to
2. to call to oneself
3. to bid to come to oneself
4. metaph.
   a. God is said to call to himself the Gentiles, aliens as
      they are from him, by inviting them, through the
      preaching of the gospel unto fellowship with himself
      in the Messiah's kingdom
   b. Christ and the Holy Spirit are said to call to
      themselves those preachers of the gospel to whom they

have decided to entrust a service having reference to the extension of the gospel

NAS Word Usage - Total: 29
call 2, called 13, calling 3, summoned 8, summoning 3

NAS Verse
Matthew 10:1; 15:10; 15:32; 18:2; 18:32; 20:25
Mark 3:13; 3:23; 6:7; 7:14; 8:1; 8:34; 10:42; 12:43; 15:44
Luke 7:19; 15:26; 16:5; 18:16
Acts 2:29; 5:40; 6:2; 13:2; 13:7; 16:10; 23:17–18; 23:23
James 5:14

sugklēronomos (Strong's Number 4789)
Parts of Speech – Noun Masculine
Phonetic Spelling: *soong-klay-ron-om'-os*
Definition

1. a fellow heir, a joint heir
2. one who obtains something assigned to himself with others, a joint participant

NAS Word Usage - Total: 4
fellow heir 1, fellow heirs 3

NAS Verse
Romans 8:17
Ephesians 3:6
Hebrews 11:9
1 Peter 3:7

APPENDIX H
New American Standard Hebrew Lexicon

The Old Testament Hebrew lexicon is based on *The New Brown-Driver-Briggs-Gesenius Hebrew-English Lexicon;* this is keyed to the *Theological Word Book of the Old Testament.* These works are in the public domain.

'âhab, 'âhêb (Strong's Number 157)
Parts of Speech – Verb
Phonetic Spelling: *aw-hab', aw-habe'*
Definition

1. to love
    a. (Qal)
        1. human love for another, includes family and sex
        2. human appetite for objects, such as food, drink, sleep, wisdom
        3. human love for or to God
        4. act of being a friend
    b. lover (participle)
    c. friend (participle)
        1. God's love toward man
        2. to individual men

3. to people of Israel
4. to righteousness
2. to like

NAS Word Usage - Total: 217
beloved 1, dearly love 1, friend 5, friends 6, love 88, loved 53, lover 1, lovers 16, loves 42, loving 2, show your love 1, shows love 1

NAS Verse
Genesis 22:2; 24:67; 25:28; 27:4; 27:9; 27:14; 29:18; 29:30; 29:32; 34:3; 37:3–4; 44:201:1; 1:8–9; 1:14–15
Exodus 20:6; 21:5
Leviticus 19:18; 19:34
Deuteronomy 4:37; 5:10; 6:5; 7:8–9; 7:13; 10:12; 10:15; 10:18–19; 11:1; 11:13; 11:22; 13:3; 15:16; 19:9; 21:15–16; 23:5; 30:6; 30:16; 30:20
Joshua 22:5; 23:11
Judges 5:31; 14:16; 16:4; 16:15
Ruth 4:15
1 Samuel 1:5; 16:21; 18:1; 18:3; 18:16; 18:20; 18:22; 18:28; 20:17
2 Samuel 1:23; 12:24; 13:1; 13:4; 13:15; 19:6
1 Kings 3:3; 5:1; 10:9; 11:1–2
2 Chronicles 2:11; 9:8; 11:21; 19:2; 20:7; 26:10
Nehemiah 1:5; 13:26
Esther 2:17; 5:10; 5:14; 6:13
Job 19:19
Psalm 4:2; 5:11; 11:5; 11:7; 26:8; 31:23; 33:5; 34:12; 37:28; 38:11; 40:16; 45:7; 47:4; 52:3–4; 69:36; 70:4; 78:68; 87:2; 88:18; 97:10; 99:4; 109:17; 116:1; 119:47–48; 119:97; 119:113; 119:119; 119:127; 119:132; 119:140; 119:159; 119:163; 119:165; 119:167; 122:6; 145:20; 146:8
Proverbs 1:22; 3:12; 4:6; 8:17; 8:21; 8:36; 9:8; 12:1; 13:24; 14:20; 15:9; 15:12; 16:13; 17:17; 17:19; 18:21; 18:24; 19:8; 20:13; 21:17; 22:11; 27:6; 29:3
Ecclesiastes 3:8; 5:10; 9:9
Song of Solomon 1:3–4; 1:7; 3:1–4

Isaiah 1:23; 41:8; 43:4; 48:14; 56:6; 56:10; 57:8; 61:8; 66:10
Jeremiah 2:25; 5:31; 8:2; 14:10; 20:4; 20:6; 22:20; 22:22; 30:14; 31:3
Lamentations 1:2; 1:19
Ezekiel 16:33; 16:36–37; 23:5; 23:9; 23:22
Daniel 9:4
Hosea 2:5; 2:7; 2:10; 2:12–13; 3:1; 4:18; 9:1; 9:10; 9:15; 10:11; 11:1;
    12:7; 14:4
Amos 4:5; 5:15
Micah 3:2; 6:8
Zechariah 8:17; 8:19; 13:6
Malachi 1:2; 2:11

bâchîyr (Strong's Number 972)
Parts of Speech – Noun Masculine
Phonetic Spelling *baw-kheer'*
Definition

chosen, choice one, chosen one, elect (of God)

NAS Word Usage - Total: 13
chosen 6, chosen ones 7

NAS Verse
2 Samuel 21:6
1 Chronicles 16:13
Psalm 89:3; 105:6; 105:43; 106:5; 106:23
Isaiah 42:1; 43:20; 5:4; 65:9; 65:15; 65:22

châshaq (Strong's Number 2836)
Parts of Speech – Verb
Phonetic Spelling: khaw-shak'
Definition

to love, be attached to, long for

chên (Strong's Number 2580)
Parts of Speech – Noun Masculine
Phonetic Spelling: *khane*
Definition

favor, grace, charm

    a. favor, grace, elegance
    b. favor, acceptance

NAS Word Usage - Total: 69
adornment 1, charm 1, charm 1, charming 1, favor 51, grace 8,
graceful 2, gracious 3, pleases 1

NAS Verse
Genesis 6:8; 18:3; 19:19; 30:27; 32:5; 33:8; 33:10; 33:15; 34:11;
    39:4; 39:21; 47:25; 47:29; 50:4
Exodus 3:21; 11:3; 12:36; 33:12–13; 33:16–17; 34:9
Numbers 11:11; 11:15; 32:5
Deuteronomy 24:1
Judges 6:17
Ruth 2:2; 2:10; 2:13
1 Samuel 1:18; 16:22; 20:3; 20:29; 25:8; 27:5
2 Samuel 14:22; 15:25; 16:4
1 Kings 11:19
Esther 2:15; 2:17; 5:2; 5:8; 7:3; 8:5
Psalm 45:2; 84:11
Proverbs 1:9; 3:4; 3:22; 3:34; 4:9; 5:19; 11:16; 13:15; 17:8; 22:1;
    22:11; 28:23; 31:30
Ecclesiastes 9:11; 10:12
Jeremiah 31:2
Nahum 3:4
Zechariah 4:7; 12:10

gâ'al (Strong's Number 1350)
Parts of Speech – Verb
Phonetic Spelling: gaw-al'
Definition

1. to redeem, act as kinsman-redeemer, avenge, revenge, ransom, do the part of a kinsman
   a. (Qal)
   b. to act as kinsman, do the part of next of kin, act as kinsman-redeemer
   c. by marrying brother's widow to beget a child for him, to redeem from slavery, to redeem land, to exact vengeance
      1. to redeem (by payment)
   d. to redeem (with God as subject)
      1. individuals from death
      2. Israel from Egyptian bondage
      3. Israel from exile
      4. (Niphal)
         a. to redeem oneself
         b. to be redeemed
2. To love, be attached to, long for

NAS Word Usage - Total: 99
avenger 13, bought back 1, buy back 1, claim 1, close relative 3, closest relative 3, closest relatives 1, ever wish to redeem 2, kinsman 2, redeem 22, redeemed 25, redeemer 1, Redeemer 18, redeems 1, relative 2, relatives 1, rescue 1, wishes to redeem 1

NAS Verse
Genesis 48:16
Exodus 6:6; 15:13
Leviticus 25:25–26; 25:30; 25:33; 25:48–49; 25:54; 27:13; 27:15; 27:19–20; 27:27–28; 27:31; 27:33
Numbers 5:8; 35:12; 35:19; 35:21; 35:24–25; 35:27
Deuteronomy 19:6; 19:12
Joshua 20:3; 20:5; 20:9

Ruth 2:20; 3:9; 3:12–13; 4:1; 4:3–4; 4:6; 4:8; 4:14
2 Samuel 14:11
1 Kings 16:11
Job 3:5; Job 19:25
Psalm 19:14; 69:18; 72:14; 74:2; 77:15; 78:35; 103:4; 106:10; 107:2;
    119:154
Proverbs 23:11
Isaiah 35:9; 41:14; 43:1; 43:14; 44:6; 44:22–24; 47:4; 48:17; 48:20;
    49:7; 49:26; 51:10; 52:3; 52:9; 54:5; 54:8; 59:20; 60:16; 62:12;
    63:9; 63:16
Jeremiah 31:11; 50:34
Lamentations 3:58
Hosea 13:14
Micah 4:10

Mishkân (Strong's Number 4908)
Parts of Speech – Noun Masculine
Phonetic Spelling: *mish-kawn'*
Definition

dwelling place, tabernacle

  a. dwelling place
  b. dwellings

NAS Word Usage - Total: 159
dwelling 1, dwelling place 8, dwelling places 9, dwellings 9, resting
place 1, tabernacle 109, tents 1, where ... dwells 1

NAS Verse
Exodus 25:9; 26:1; 26:6–7; 26:12–13; 26:15; 26:17–18; 26:20;
    26:22–23; 26:26–27; 26:30; 26:35; 27:9; 27:19; 35:11; 35:15;
    35:18; 36:8; 36:13–14; 36:20; 36:22–23; 36:25; 36:27–28;
    36:31–32; 38:20–21; 38:31; 39:32–33; 39:40; 40:2; 40:5–6;
    40:9; 40:17–19; 40:21–22; 40:24; 40:28–29; 40:33–36; 40:38
Leviticus 8:10; 15:31; 17:4; 26:11

Numbers 1:50–51; 1:53; 3:7–8; 3:23; 3:25–26; 3:29; 3:35–36; 3:38;
   4:16; 4:25–26; 4:31; 5:17; 7:1; 7:3; 9:15; 9:18–20; 9:22; 10:11;
   10:17; 10:21; 16:9; 16:24; 16:27; 17:13; 19:13; 24:5; 31:30; 31:47
Joshua 22:19; 22:29
2 Samuel 7:6
1 Chronicles 6:32; 6:48; 16:39; 17:5; 21:29; 23:26
2 Chronicles 1:5; 29:6
Job 18:21; 21:28; 39:6
Psalm 26:8; 43:3; 46:4; 49:11; 74:7; 78:28; 78:60; 84:1; 87:2;
   132:5; 132:7
Song of Solomon 1:8
Isaiah 22:16; 32:18; 54:2
Jeremiah 9:19; 30:18; 51:30
Ezekiel 25:4; 37:27
Habakkuk 1:6

Pâdâh (Strong's Number 6299)
Parts of Speech – Verb
Phonetic Spelling: *paw-daw'*
Definition

to ransom, redeem, rescue, deliver

   a. to ransom
   b. to be ransomed
   c. to allow one to be ransomed
   d. redeemed

NAS Word Usage - Total: 59
any means redeem 1, ransom 4, ransomed 7, redeem 24, redeemed 18,
redeems 1, redemption price 1, rescued 1, surely redeem 1, way been
redeemed 1

NAS Verse
Exodus 13:13; 13:15; 21:8; 34:20
Leviticus 19:20; 27:27; 27:29

Numbers 3:46; 3:49; 3:51; 18:15–17
Deuteronomy 7:8; 9:26; 13:5; 15:15; 21:8; 24:18
1 Samuel 14:45
2 Samuel 4:9; 7:23
1 Kings 1:29
1 Chronicles 17:21
Nehemiah 1:10
Job 5:20; 6:23; 33:28
Psalm 25:22; 26:11; 31:5; 34:22; 44:26; 49:7; 49:15; 55:18; 69:18;
    71:23; 78:42; 119:134; 130:8
Isaiah 1:27; 29:22; 35:10; 51:11
Jeremiah 15:21; 31:11
Hosea 7:13; 13:14
Micah 6:4
Zechariah 10:8

shâmayim, shâmeh (Strong's Number 8064)
Parts of Speech – Noun Masculine
Phonetic Spelling: *shaw-mah'-yim, shaw-meh'*
Definition

heaven, heavens, sky

    a.   visible heavens, sky
        1.   s abode of the stars
        2.   as the visible universe, the sky, atmosphere, etc.
    b.   Heaven (as the abode of God)

NAS Word Usage - Total: 411
astrologers* 1, compass 1, earth 1, heaven 191, heaven and the
highest 2, heaven and the highest heavens 1, heaven of heavens 1,
heavenly 3, heavens 151, heavens and the highest 1, highest heaven 1,
highest heaven 1, highest heavens 4, horizons 1, other* 1, sky 50

NAS Verse
Genesis 1:1; 1:8–9; 1:14–15; 1:17; 1:20; 1:26; 1:28; 1:30; 2:1; 2:4;

2:19–20; 6:7; 6:17; 7:3; 7:11; 7:19; 7:23; 8:2; 9:2; 11:4; 14:19;
    14:22; 15:5; 19:24; 21:17; 22:11; 22:15; 22:17; 24:3; 24:7; 26:4;
    27:28; 27:39; 28:12; 28:17; 49:25

Exodus 9:8; 9:10; 9:22–23; 10:21–22; 16:4; 17:14; 20:4; 20:11;
    20:22; 24:10; 31:17; 32:13

Leviticus 26:19

Deuteronomy 1:10; 1:28; 2:25; 3:24; 4:11; 4:17; 4:19; 4:26; 4:32;
    4:36; 4:39; 5:8; 7:24; 9:1; 9:14; 10:14; 10:22; 11:11; 11:17; 11:21;
    17:3; 25:19; 26:15; 28:12; 28:23–24; 28:26; 28:62; 29:20; 30:4;
    30:12; 30:19; 31:28; 32:1; 32:40; 33:13; 33:26; 33:28

Joshua 2:11; 8:20; 10:11; 10:13

Judges 5:4; 5:20; 13:20; 20:40

1 Samuel 2:10; 5:12; 17:44; 17:46

2 Samuel 18:9; 21:10; 22:8; 22:10

1 Kings 8:22–23; 8:27; 8:30; 8:32; 8:34–36; 8:39; 8:43; 8:45;
    8:49; 8:54; 14:11; 16:4; 18:45; 21:24; 22:19

2 Kings 1:10; 1:12; 1:14; 2:1; 2:11; 7:2; 7:19; 14:27; 17:16; 19:15;
    21:3; 21:5; 23:4–5

1 Chronicles 16:26; 16:31; 21:16; 21:26; 27:23; 29:11

2 Chronicles 2:6; 2:12; 6:13–14; 6:18; 6:21; 6:23; 6:25–27; 6:30;
    6:33; 6:35; 6:39; 7:1; 7:13–14; 18:18; 20:6; 28:9; 30:27; 32:20;
    33:3; 33:5; 36:23

Ezra 1:2; 9:6

Nehemiah 1:4–5; 1:9; 2:4; 2:20; 9:6; 9:13; 9:15; 9:23; 9:27–28

Job 1:16; 2:12; 9:8; 11:8; 12:7; 14:12; 15:15; 16:19; 20:6; 20:27;
    22:12; 22:14; 26:11; 26:13; 28:21; 28:24; 35:5; 35:11; 37:3;
    38:29; 38:33; 38:37; 41:11

Psalm 2:4; 8:1; 8:3; 8:8; 11:4; 14:2; 18:9; 18:13; 19:1; 19:6; 20:6; 33:6;
    33:13; 36:5; 50:4; 50:6; 53:2; 57:3; 57:5; 57:10–11; 68:8; 68:33;
    69:34; 73:9; 73:25; 76:8; 78:23–24; 78:26; 79:2; 80:14; 85:11;
    89:2; 89:5; 89:11; 89:29; 96:5; 96:11; 97:6; 102:19; 102:25; 103:11;
    103:19; 104:2; 104:12; 105:40; 107:26; 108:4–5; 113:4; 113:6;
    115:3; 115:15–16; 119:89; 121:2; 123:1; 124:8; 134:3; 135:6;
    136:5; 136:26; 139:8; 144:5; 146:6; 147:8; 148:1; 148:4; 148:13

Proverbs 3:19; 8:27; 23:5; 25:3; 30:4; 30:19

Ecclesiastes 1:13; 2:3; 3:1; 5:2; 10:20

Isaiah 1:2; 13:5; 13:13; 34:4–5; 37:16; 40:12; 40:22; 42:5; 44:23–
24; 45:8; 45:12; 45:18; 47:13; 48:13; 49:13; 50:3; 51:6; 51:13;
51:16; 55:9–10; 63:15; 64:1; 65:17; 66:1; 66:22
Jeremiah 2:12; 4:23; 4:25; 4:28; 7:18; 7:33; 8:2; 8:7; 9:10; 10:2; 10:12–
13; 14:22; 15:3; 16:4; 19:7; 19:13; 23:24; 31:37; 32:17; 33:22;
33:25; 34:20; 44:17–19; 44:25; 49:36; 51:9; 51:15–16; 51:48; 51:53
Lamentations 2:1; 3:41; 3:50; 3:66; 4:19
Ezekiel 1:1; 8:3; 29:5; 31:6; 31:13; 32:4; 32:7–8; 38:20
Daniel 8:8; 8:10; 9:12; 11:4; 12:7
Hosea 2:18; 2:21; 4:3; 7:12
Joel 2:10; 2:30; 3:16
Amos 9:2; 9:6
Jonah 1:9
Nahum 3:16
Habakkuk 3:3
Zephaniah 1:3; 1:5
Haggai 1:10; 2:6; 2:21
Zechariah 2:6; 5:9; 6:5; 8:12; 12:1
Malachi 3:10

Shaba` (Strong's Number 7650)
Parts of Speech – Verb
Phonetic Spelling: *shä·bah'*
Definition

1. to swear, adjure
2. (Qal) sworn (participle)
   a. (Niphal)
   b. to swear, take an oath
      1. to swear (of Jehovah by Himself)
      2. to curse
      3. (Hiphil)
   c. to cause to take an oath
      1. to adjure

NAS Word Usage - Total: 188
adjure 6, curse 1, exchanged oaths 1, made a covenant 1, made an oath 1, promised an oath 1, promised them by oath 1, put the under oath 1, put them under oath 1, solemn 1, solemnly swear 1, strictly put 1, swear 40, swearer 1, swearing 1, swears 6, swore 62, sworn 41, take an oath 2, take the oath 1, take oath 1, takes 1, took an oath 3, took the oath 1, under oath 3, used 1, vow 1, vowed 6

tôrâh (Strong's Number 8451)
Parts of Speech – Noun Feminine
Phonetic Spelling: *to-raw'*
Definition

law, direction, instruction

- a. instruction, direction (human or divine)
  1. body of prophetic teaching
  2. instruction in Messianic age
  3. body of priestly direction or instruction
  4. body of legal directives
- b. law
  1. law of the burnt offering
  2. of special law, codes of law
- c. custom, manner
- d. the Deuteronomic or Mosaic Law

NAS Word Usage - Total: 220
custom 1, instruction 10, instructions 1, Law 1, law 188, laws 10, ruling 1, teaching 7, teachings 1

NAS Verse
Genesis 26:5
Exodus 12:49; 13:9; 16:4; 16:28; 18:16; 18:20; 24:12
Leviticus 6:9; 6:14; 6:25; 7:1; 7:7; 7:11; 7:37; 11:46; 12:7; 13:59; 14:2; 14:32; 14:54; 14:57; 15:32; 26:46
Numbers 5:29–30; 6:13; 6:21; 15:16; 15:29; 19:2; 19:14; 31:21

Deuteronomy 1:5; 4:8; 4:44; 17:11; 17:18–19; 27:3; 27:8; 27:26;
  28:58; 28:61; 29:21; 29:29; 30:10; 31:9; 31:11–12; 31:24;
  31:26; 32:46; 33:4; 33:10
 Joshua 1:7–8; 8:31–32; 8:34; 22:5; 23:6; 24:26
2 Samuel 7:19
1 Kings 2:3
2 Kings 10:31; 14:6; 17:13; 17:34; 17:37; 21:8; 22:8; 22:11; 23:24–25
1 Chronicles 16:40; 22:12
2 Chronicles 6:16; 12:1; 14:4; 15:3; 17:9; 19:10; 23:18; 25:4; 30:16;
  31:3–4; 31:21; 33:8; 34:14–15; 34:19; 35:26
Ezra 3:2; 7:6; 7:10; 10:3
Nehemiah 8:1–3; 8:7–9; 8:13–14; 8:18; 9:3; 9:13–14; 9:26; 9:29;
  9:34; 10:28–29; 10:34; 10:36; 12:44; 13:3
Job 22:22
Psalm 1:2; 19:7; 37:31; 40:8; 78:1; 78:5; 78:10; 89:30; 94:12;
  105:45; 119:1; 119:18; 119:29; 119:34; 119:44; 119:51; 119:53;
  119:55; 119:61; 119:70; 119:72; 119:77; 119:85; 119:92; 119:97;
  119:109; 119:113; 119:126; 119:136; 119:142; 119:150; 119:153;
  119:163; 119:165; 119:174
Proverbs 1:8; 3:1; 4:2; 6:20; 6:23; 7:2; 13:14; 28:4; 28:7; 28:9;
  29:18; 31:26
Isaiah 1:10; 2:3; 5:24; 8:16; 8:20; 24:5; 30:9; 42:4; 42:21; 42:24;
  51:4; 51:7
Jeremiah 2:8; 6:19; 8:8; 9:13; 16:11; 18:18; 26:4; 31:33; 32:23;
  44:10; 44:23
Lamentations 2:9
Ezekiel 7:26; 22:26; 43:11–12; 44:5; 44:24
Daniel 9:10–11; 9:13
Hosea 4:6; 8:1; 8:12
Amos 2:4
Micah 4:2
Habakkuk 1:4
Zephaniah 3:4
Haggai 2:11
Zechariah 7:12
Malachi 2:6–9; 4:4

BIBLIOGRAPHY

Blum, Edwin A. "John." *The Bible Knowledge Commentary: New Testament Edition*. Colorado Springs: David C. Cook, 1983.

Brown, Driver, Briggs, and Gesenius, *The NAS Old Testament Hebrew Lexicon* http://www.biblestudytools.com/lexicons/hebrew/nas/, 2010.

Chafer, Lewis Sperry. *Systematic Theology*. Dallas: Dallas Theological Seminary Press, 1948.

Geisler, Norman L. "Colossians." *The Bible Knowledge Commentary: New Testament Edition*. Colorado Springs: David C. Cook, 1983.

Hirsch, Frank E. "Inherit." *Eerdman's International Standard Bible Encyclopedia*. Grand Rapids: William B. Eerdmans Publishing Company, 1988.

Hoehner, Harold W. "Ephesians." *The Bible Knowledge Commentary: New Testament Edition*. Colorado Springs: David C. Cook, 1983.

McKim, Donald K. "Inherit." *Eerdman's International Standard*

Bible Encyclopedia. Grand Rapids: William B. Eerdmans Publishing Company, 1988.

Pentecost, Dwight J. "Daniel." *The Bible Knowledge Commentary: Old Testament Edition.* Colorado Springs: David C. Cook, 1983.

Scofield, C. I. "Hebrews." *The Scofield Study Bible and Commentary.* New York: Oxford University Press, 1945.

Stedman, Ray C. *Our Riches in Christ: Discovering the Believer's Inheritance in Ephesians.* http://www.raystedman.org/ephesians/richesinchrist.html#anchor18617, 2010.

Strong, James. *Strong's Exhaustive Concordance of the Bible Concordance.* Nashville: Crusade Bible Publishers, Inc.

The NAS New Testament Greek Lexicon http://www.biblestudytools.com/lexicons/greek/nas/, 2010.

Westerholm, Steven. "Tabernacle." *Eerdman's International Standard Bible Encyclopedia.* Grand Rapids: William B. Eerdmans Publishing Company, 1988.

Wilson, Macartney J. "Angel." *Eerdman's International Standard Bible Encyclopedia.* Grand Rapids: William B. Eerdmans Publishing Company, 1988.

ABOUT THE AUTHOR

Award Winning Author, Judy Azar Leblanc is an internationally published author of several other works. A Graduate of San Jose State University, she currently resides in East Texas where she devotes her time to writing.